The StartUp Kit

The StartUp Kit

Everything you need to start a small business

Emma Jones

Enterprise Nation

An Enterprise Nation book
www.enterprisenation.com

With

HARRIMAN HOUSE LTD
3 Viceroy Court
Bedford Road
Petersfield
Hampshire
GU2 3LJ
GREAT BRITAIN

Tel: +44 (0)1730 233870

Email: **enquiries@harriman-house.com**
Website: **www.harriman-house.com**

First published in Great Britain in 2013. This edition published in 2020.

Paperback 978-0-85719-810-5 Ebook 978-0-85719-811-2

Copyright © Emma Jones

British Library Cataloguing in Publication Data
A CIP catalogue record for this book can be obtained from the British Library.

Contents

Who This Kit is For   vi

About the Author   vii

About Start Up Loans   viii

Foreword
by Richard Bearman, Managing Director, Start Up Loans, British Business Bank   ix

Let's Get Started   1

PART I. Prepare   3

   1. Coming Up With an Idea   5

   2. Research the Market   16

   3. Write a Plan   22

   4. Register the Company   28

   5. Protect the Brand   35

   6. Take Care of Household Admin   37

   7. Your Tech Setup   42

   8. Working 5 to 9   51

   9. Starting on a Budget and Straightforward Finance   55

PART II. Launch   63

   10. Create a First Impression   65

   11. Make Sales   84

   12. Make Some Noise!   96

PART III. Grow   119

   13. Attract Customers Back   121

   14. Focus On What You Do Best and Outsource the Rest   125

   15. Keep the Business in Balance   131

   16. Support   136

The Best of Luck   138

How Enterprise Nation Can Help   139

With Thanks   140

☆ Who This Kit is For

*T*he *StartUp Kit* is for anyone considering or starting a business. You may have been thinking about how you can make a living from a particular passion, hobby or skill. Perhaps you're working a day job and already making sales on the side – now you want to take it to the next level. Maybe you haven't hit upon the right idea yet; you just know in your heart that you want to be your own boss.

This kit offers all the tools and tips you need to succeed. It'll help you find an idea, spot a gap in the market and start your own small business. Doing so will be one of the best moves you've ever made!

About the Author

Emma Jones is a business expert, author and founder of small business network Enterprise Nation. Her books include *Working 5 to 9*, *Go Global: How to take your business to the world* and *Turn Your Talent Into a Business*.

Following a five-year career at an international accounting firm, Emma started her first business at 27. That business was sold 18 months later, and the experience led to Emma's next venture, Enterprise Nation.

Its website (**www.enterprisenation.com**) was launched in 2006 and became the most popular site for home business owners in the UK, attracting over 100,000 visitors each month.

In the past decade, Enterprise Nation has grown into the UK's most active small business community. Founders, owners and entrepreneurs find help and support on its website, in its books and at live events. The company has a membership scheme, which helps members promote their business, take their venture to the next level and have their views represented to government.

In 2011, Emma was a co-founder of StartUp Britain, a national campaign to encourage more people to start a business.

Emma was awarded an MBE for services to enterprise in July 2012 and appointed to co-chair the Prime Minister's small business council in 2018.

About Start Up Loans

This StartUp Kit is produced in partnership with Start Up Loans.

The Start Up Loans Company was established in September 2012, with a mission to help new and early stage UK businesses access affordable finance and mentoring support. The company works with a national network of delivery partners who are based across England, Wales, Scotland and Northern Ireland. In addition to helping applicants prepare their business plan and cash flow forecast, delivery partners are responsible for assessing final applications and providing ongoing mentoring support to successful applicants.

The Start Up Loans Company has backed over 60,000 businesses and lent half a billion pounds. The scheme has had a transformative impact on the lives of thousands of individuals, local communities and the nation as a whole. For every £1 invested in the scheme, £3.30 of value is delivered back into the UK economy.

Loans | Mentoring | Support

Part of the British Business Bank

Foreword
by Richard Bearman, Managing Director, Start Up Loans, British Business Bank

The benefits of owning your own business can be very attractive. Working for yourself means more independence, having more flexibility and the opportunity to follow your passion. The UK is a great place to start a business, reflected in a country-wide business creation rate of over 1,000 a day.

My own passion for supporting small businesses and entrepreneurs comes from working with the sector for over 20 years. During my time spent as Head of Small Business at HSBC UK, I saw first-hand the trials and tribulations, ambitions and successes of entrepreneurs up and down the country.

And having recently been appointed as Managing Director of Start Up Loans, part of the British Business Bank, it's been great to see government funding being put to good use in encouraging and supporting entrepreneurship. Working with our nationwide network of delivery partners, we've lent more than £500m, through over 64,000 loans, since the programme was established in 2012.

But finance isn't the only ingredient for business success. At Start Up Loans, and at the British Business Bank more widely, we believe strongly in the benefits of making sure that there are other resources that businesses can call upon to help them along the road to success. The mentoring we offer to our Start Up Loans recipients provides invaluable support in their first year, and our popular online Finance Hub helps businesses to explore further the finance options that might best suit their needs.

It goes without saying that the number one priority for any entrepreneur is, of course, to start and run their business, and therefore any guide which helps them to do so needs to be quickly and easily accessible, clear and user-friendly.

That's why Start Up Loans is delighted to be sponsoring this new Enterprise Nation *StartUp Kit* – a valuable resource that covers everything you need to know about launching your own business in a simple and easy-to-understand way.

I hope you find it a useful tool to help you succeed in your new venture.

Richard Bearman

Managing Director, Start Up Loans, British Business Bank

Let's Get Started

There has never been a better time to start a business and in 2019 record numbers of people did just that. According to Companies House, over 500,000 people formed a limited company in the space of 12 months. A survey called the Global Entrepreneurship Monitor revealed the highest number of people starting a business since research began in 1999, and this is mirrored in data from the Department for Business, Innovation and Skills showing the number of small businesses having increased to 5.7 million – another record high.

Why is this happening? Simple: because it's now perfectly possible to start and grow a successful business

- in your spare time
- from home
- on a budget
- with help from friends and others.

In this kit, I'll show you how it's done.

People in their thousands are spotting gaps in the market or turning their hobbies into a successful venture. They are embracing free or low-cost technology to promote themselves and make sales, with a good number of these sales coming from overseas customers. Having access to the internet means you can start a business on a Monday and be trading with the world by Wednesday.

The start-up companies profiled in this book discuss how they got going and how they accessed the invaluable support that's helped them along the way. They are selling everything from bath scrubs to dog hotels, healthy cookies and digital services. Their products may be different, but the owners of these businesses all talk about the opportunities available to them and the joy of having the freedom to work how and where they like. Many started in employment. A good number are already going global.

If you'd like to experience the same sense of independence and excitement, all you have to do is follow some basic steps: come up with an idea, do some research and marketing, offer good customer service – and you're in business!

In the following pages I'll walk you through everything that's involved in doing this successfully.

Emma Jones | @emmaljones

PART I. Prepare

With any undertaking, preparation is key. Whether baking a cake, going on a date or heading on holiday, time is given over to research and preparation. Starting a business is no different. Dedicate time to coming up with an idea, ensuring it's viable, and registering with the relevant bodies. These are the base ingredients required for a successful enterprise!

1. Coming Up With an Idea

Ingredient number one: a business idea! Many people tell me they would like to start a business but what's holding them back is not having an idea. It's easy to come up with one. Ask yourself these three questions:

1. Is there a gap in the market?

Have you tried to buy something that you just can't find? Could others be looking for the same thing? If so, this presents a market opportunity. It was a gap in the market that encouraged Emma Cranstoun to leave a job for a life of entrepreneurship.

2. What is my passion/hobby/skill?

Many people are turning what they love into a way of making a living. Best of all, when you work on what you enjoy, doing it never really feels like work. Are you a dab hand at design? Have an eye for photography? A head for figures? These skills and hobbies can easily be turned into a business.

3. Is there something someone else is doing that I can do better myself?

If you've bought something and been unimpressed, why not step in, set up a business, and provide a better offer? Many good ideas stem from spotting products and services that can simply be improved upon or offered for less.

* * *

Your idea will develop over time. Don't be surprised if in 12 months' time it looks different to when you started out. This is okay. Business ideas tend to get refined over time; your offer will get sharper the more experience you gain in the marketplace. What's important is to get started with the beginnings of an idea – there'll be time to develop it as you get feedback from customers and input from others.

CASE STUDY

Name: **Emma Cranstoun** | Business: **Scrubbington's**

A lot of people have their big idea in the shower. For Emma Cranstoun it was her son's bathtime that provided inspiration:

> "I was washing my son in the bath when he was about five years old and thinking: 'why am I still using a product with a picture of a baby on it? And – more importantly – why isn't he washing himself?'

> "I started looking around for bath and shower products for kids. There wasn't anything, so with my friend Karen we thought maybe we could create our own. That was about four years ago now and it's been a rollercoaster ever since!"

The two friends wanted a natural product kids could use themselves. But didn't know anything about product design or manufacturing.

> "The start of the business was really exciting and I loved the actual making of the range. Our chemist was really helpful and a great resource to start us up. We funded ourselves for the first year, so it meant we had to beg, borrow and barter wherever we could. But that's the fun of it and I've really enjoyed working closely with my friend Karen – we make a great team."

The next step was to get a listing in a retailer. The game changing moment happened at a 'Meet the Buyer' event organised by Enterprise Nation. A year later Scrubbington's was stocked in Boots.

> "Being on the enormous Boots' head office site and pitching Scrubbington's felt a bit like a dream. We only had five minutes to pitch to them. We learnt that we had to be really short and explain really quickly what makes our products different from everything

else. We also learnt to back ourselves a bit more as we really do know our stuff – that's hard to remember when you get stuck in the day-to-day running of the business."

The ethos of the brand was important to cut through the noise. Natural products are a big trend across food and personal care.

"All of our products are 98% natural which Boots loved. We were also talking to them about creating a new sub-category of 'Children' rather than 'Babies', which they liked as it means there are more parents staying in the baby aisle for longer. We also talked about gender-neutral marketing, which is really important to the marketers and mums in us. A lot of this category has a 'pink one' and a 'blue one' and we didn't want to be anything like that."

Getting the Boots listing meant developing their capabilities.

"We had to get more serious about stock control and manufacturing. We have a mega-spreadsheet, which helps us to manage our forecasting and componentry ordering. We now have a sales person, a brilliant social media manager and monthly board meetings to keep us on track. We still oscillate between fear and joy on a nearly daily basis but we wouldn't change a thing!"

Scrubbington's is now listed in 400 Boots stores as well as Ocado, Booths and online with Amazon.

50 ideas for businesses

These are all ideas and businesses we have seen and profiled on Enterprise Nation. Many of them started as '5 to 9' businesses. In other words, a business started whilst the entrepreneur was in full-time study or employment. More on that later!

Blogger

Vlogger

Social media adviser

eBay trader

Online store owner

Giftware maker

Giftware seller

Artisan

Cupcake maker

Cosmetics producer

Hair and make-up artist

Origami artist

Picture artist

Furniture maker

Jewellery designer

Footwear designer

Fashion designer

Clothing producer

Toymaker

Party organiser

DJ

Musician

Magician

Beer producer

Events organiser

Wedding planner

Mystery shopper

Image consultant

Fitness adviser

Personal trainer

Photographer

Accountant

Lawyer

Translator

IT services

App developer

Software developer

Print and web designer

Network marketer

Pet care & doggy treats

Product manufacturer

E-learning provider

Facebook developer

Magazine publisher

T-shirt maker

Papercrafter

Dance instructor

Perfumer

Balloon decorator

Streetfood caterer

There are so many possibilities. You might even have too many ideas. In which case, don't be afraid to spend some time on all of them and, wherever possible, let the customer decide – try them out in small ways and see what gets the warmest response.

Niche is nice

When coming up with your idea, bear in mind that niche businesses are often ideal. Meeting the needs of a very well-defined audience helps keep your efforts focused and your offering clear in a crowded market. It also means success should naturally consolidate itself. So rather than just selling clothes, why not become the go-to place for men's blazers, and instead of offering food to suit all palates, how about re-inventing pizza so it offers a balanced meal to consumers interested in healthy eating?

With a niche business:

- **you keep marketing costs low**, as your audience is well-defined; you know where your audience are and understand the kind of marketing messages to which they will respond

- **customer loyalty remains high**, as you become the expert in your field or the only provider of certain products; customers will want to stay with you and benefit from the specialist product or service you offer.

> **FRIENDS AND FAMILY FOCUS GROUP:** *Talk to family and friends and ask them where they think your talents lie. They might just help you discover your business idea in an area you hadn't thought of.*

Whatever the idea, good ones tend be based on what you enjoy, what people will buy and something that improves on what's already available. Think about how you can fashion your idea so it has a clear purpose for a clearly defined audience.

PJ Farr's business is a niche one serving the construction industry. This focus has helped him rapidly build revenue and credibility, with support from others.

CASE STUDY

Name: **PJ Farr** | Business: **UK Connect**

PJ Farr recalls how he was fascinated by the Army's ability to deploy to some of the most remote locations in the world and quickly maintain reliable and secure connectivity. When it became time to leave soldiering, PJ took this as inspiration for his business and, six years on, UK Connect has become the nation's leading provider of communication solutions to the construction industry.

PJ first experienced Army life as a child, travelling with his father around the world to new postings; a 'pad brat' as PJ describes himself. The Army was the natural career choice for PJ, he explains:

> "I joined the 2nd Battalion The Princess of Wales's Royal Regiment (Tigers) after I was kindly asked to leave school early. I joined this regiment because it is my local regiment and because of its amazing history and the opportunities it would give me. Coming from an army background myself it was obvious to me that this is what I would do and I also felt a sense of pride serving for my country and my mates who joined with me.

> "I started my Army career in Catterick on the Combat Infantryman course before being posted to Cyprus for just under 2 years as part of the TRB. I then moved to London where I was very involved in the London 2012 Olympics before being part of the royal wedding, which was a fantastic day and an honour."

At the age of 25, PJ decided that the full service wouldn't be for him and it was time to take what he'd learned in the Army and try his hand in the civilian workplace. PJ admitted to struggling to settle in employed roles, and he began to build on his communication skills acquired in the Army.

> "Business was something I had always wanted to do, and the opportunity presented itself after finding it difficult to make best use of my transferable skills within civilian job roles. I set up the business – originally named Countrywide Telecoms – to provide communication services to the construction industry. For the first time, sites could launch with full broadband and phone service in under 10 days using our innovative product we called Site Connect."

PJ was one of the first entrepreneurs that X-Forces Enterprise (XFE) supported. He started the business with just £1,100 in the bank, but thanks to a Start Up Loan to buy a van and tools, PJ began trading in January 2013. The business scaled up rapidly and UK Connect is now a multimillion-pound business that, in 2019, employs 25 people and is growing continuously, deploying broadband solutions to hundreds of construction sites across the UK every month.

PJ prides himself on supporting the veteran community and UK Connect is a member of the Armed Forces Covenant and has employed many veterans in the past and continues to do so today.

XFE has advised and mentored PJ since the company's launch, thanks to a scheme supported by the Start Up Loans Company and The Royal British Legion. Through XFE's 'Big Business Supporting Small Business' scheme, UK Connect was introduced to Scott Gardener, CEO at Cisco as a corporate mentor and partner, which has developed into a mutually positive relationship. PJ said:

> "Having the support of X-Forces has been fantastic. UK Connect was one of the first to be supported so we have been on a similar journey of growth. The main thing that X-Forces did for me was give me the first big push to get going and help me to identify a support network I could lean on. XFE's mentoring has been incredibly valuable. I felt they understood my needs better than a civvy organisation and helped me to apply the transferable skills from my time in the military.

> "I found setting the business up to be fairly simple but running the business to be a different thing all together. I had to get my head around VAT, Corporation tax and all the other elements you're not aware of. In the beginning, I found myself working in the business a lot and not on the business. Being aware of this and channelling my time and efforts has made a real difference to growth."

UK Connect currently looks after thousands of construction sites across the UK with its flagship super-fast site broadband service, Site Connect. It was this exceptional growth that attracted the attention of the London Stock Exchange Group in 2018. PJ was invited to join their Elite Programme, on which he receives coaching and support to nurture his business's potential towards listing on the exchange. UK Connect was recognised by the Soldiering On Awards, winning the Business of the Year – Scale Up Award 2019.

Maximising these platforms and introductions, UK Connect has been collaborating with the London Stock Exchange Group and Cisco to develop pioneering, innovative technologies for the construction industry, improving sustainability and productivity in the industry.

PJ is now enjoying family life in Guildford, with his wife Zoey, and son Alfie. Upon meeting PJ, his energy and drive is abundantly obvious, and it is no surprise that his business has been a success. PJ explains that his ambition doesn't rest here:

> "UK Connect is now a national multimillion-pound company. This is something I could only have dreamed of. I'm now looking at launching my next business using the skills I have learnt from my current business. Running a business that works whilst also giving me time to spend with my young family.

> "As a former solider, I bump into people all the time who did not join the Army but tell me they wish they had done. When I ask them why they did not join up, the answer may be different each time but its normally down to just one thing: fear of the unknown and being out of their comfort zone. The same thing can be said about running a business. If you don't do it, you will regret it.

> "In the military, we can draw confidence from the fact that we have experienced greater challenges and risk in the past. I would advise that, if you really do want to own a business, then go for it but don't do it alone. Ask for help as there is a lot of it out there."

Ren Kapur MBE, XFE CEO and Founder, comments on PJ's progress:

"One word comes to mind immediately when I'm asked about PJ: energy. He positively buzzes with energy for business and progress, it's infectious.

"He is absolutely right when he says we've been on a journey together; PJ was one of the first ex-military entrepreneurs that came to us when I started X-Forces back in 2012. I was struck by his focus, determination and straight-talking, which we know is characteristic across our 1500 beneficiaries, and I am certain that this pragmatic approach is at the heart of PJ's success.

"At XFE we have worked incredibly hard to build a supportive network around our entrepreneurs, from big business, government and charity. PJ has fully embraced our mentoring programme and the opportunities within this wide-reaching network to support UK Connect's growth. The power of networking is recognised in business, and we are delighted to enable big doors to open, facilitating positive introductions and profile-raising platforms for energetic entrepreneurs such as PJ."

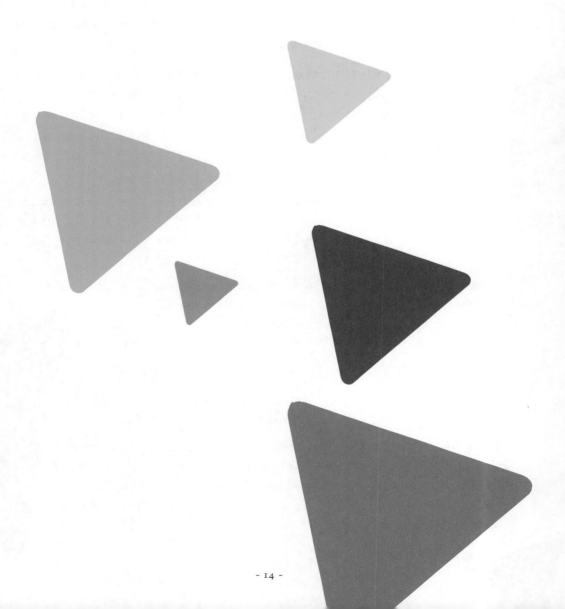

An idea as part of the package

If you're not able to settle on a viable idea of your own, consider buying into someone else's idea. You can do so through a franchise or signing up as a party-plan consultant and/or direct sales agent. Benefit from being your own boss whilst having the support of a central team and the proven idea that comes with it!

Here are a few top franchise or party-plan opportunities:

- The Pampered Chef | **www.pamperedchef.com**
- Avon | **www.avon.uk.com**
- Kleeneze | **www.kleeneze.com**
- Neal's Yard | **www.nealsyardremedies.com**
- Maid2Clean | **www.maid2clean.co.uk**
- Razzamataz | **www.razzamataz.co.uk**
- Travel Counsellors | **www.travelcounsellors.co.uk**
- Tatty Bumpkin | **www.tattybumpkin.com**
- Barrett & Coe | **www.barrettandcoe.co.uk**
- Barking Mad | **www.barkingmad.uk.com**
- PyjamaDrama | **www.pyjamadrama.com**
- Usborne Books | **www.usborne.com**

Useful links

- Direct Selling Association | **www.dsa.org.uk**
- British Franchise Association | **www.thebfa.org**

2. Research the Market

You have your idea. Turning it into a business requires some research, followed by a straightforward exercise in building that research into a plan. Here's how to go about it.

First, research your potential customers, the competition and a price point by visiting competitors' sites, online trade sites/forums, reading reports, and seeking intelligence from experts.

Look for data and comments that will answer the following questions:

- What is the number of potential customers you can serve, and how do these customers like to be served?

- What are their core characteristics and spending patterns, and who are their key influencers?

- Who is currently serving your market?

- Where are your potential customers going for their goods and services?

- What do they like about what they're getting and, more importantly, what do they dislike (as this opens up opportunities for you to improve on the status quo)?

- In view of the above, what price can you charge for your product/service?

Price yourself at a rate that's competitive with other providers in the market, that takes into account the amount of time, personal service and added value you offer, and that will turn a profit at the end of the day.

WHAT AM I WORTH? *How much do you think customers or clients would pay for your product or service? Take a look at how similar offerings are priced and talk to people about how much they'd be willing to pay. Then talk to suppliers to check you can source materials and deliver at a price that covers your costs. Since starting a business from home (which I recommend you do!) will save you lots of money, you can pass some of these savings onto your customers. It will give you an edge over other businesses. But don't undercharge for the expertise and knowledge you offer. Only consider charging less for work that will reflect well on your business and boost your reputation, perhaps in the media or with a particularly important customer.*

You can also source primary, or firsthand, data by conducting a survey or posing questions on social media channels.

Survey tools

* SurveyMonkey | **www.surveymonkey.com**
* Wufoo | **www.wufoo.com**

Social media channels

* Twitter | **www.twitter.com**
* Facebook | **www.facebook.com**
* LinkedIn | **www.linkedin.com**
* Instagram | **www.instagram.com**

Or, of course, you can hit the streets with a clipboard!

CASE STUDY

Name: **Meenesh Mistry** | Business: **Wholey Moly**

Meenesh always wanted to start a business. In the end, it was the afternoon lull that gave him the inspiration needed to make the leap.

> "My background is working in corporate offices. Most people get that afternoon slump and reach for a coffee. I always found there were lots of treats like cakes or doughnuts. They're high in sugar and calories and not much else. They give you a pick me up and then you go back to zero. I do want something sweet with my afternoon tea or coffee, but why does it have to be high in sugar and calories?"

He started working on potential replacements. The idea evolved into a flapjack and then a cookie.

> "My wife and I started off together in our kitchen. I was pushing it because I always had the motivation to start a business. She was helping me understand how to bake because I had never done it before. We were Googling recipes and then changing a whole bunch of things."

Meenesh listened to start-up podcasts and read lots of books. But he learnt the most from building his network at events and trying to force people to meet him for a coffee.

> "It's not for everybody but one thing I did was to work for Oppo Ice Cream. They have brand ambassadors that do flyering and sampling. It's normally students. I was a 32-year-old with a wife and a baby.

> "The experience was a million times more valuable than a book, a podcast or networking event. It opened my eyes to things that might have been below me before when I was working at a desk, jobs like flyering. It helped to get a feel for what it would be like and change my mindset from the corporate office to doing any job that needs to be done."

Eric Ries' book *The Lean Startup* aims to help tech start-ups innovate. But Meenesh applied the philosophy to his recipes, making hundreds of batches.

"It began getting quite scientific. Pulling out a spreadsheet – I'm an accountant, so I love spreadsheets – to record everything. We would test things like reducing the sugar by one, two and three grams to see what the difference was.

"It was going from a scattergun approach to making a hypothesis and changing one thing at a time. What different component changes what?"

The next step was to try the recipes in a commercial kitchen, which he hired by the day to do more testing.

"We were taking them into the office and giving them to friends and family. Everyone liked them. But people on the street paying for it is a different thing. Just before I jacked in my job we did markets to see if there was demand.

"On our first market all of our cookies crumbled in transit. It was a huge learning. We were using rapeseed oil. We changed it to coconut oil, which hardens at room temperature."

Wholey Moly launched 14 months' ago with a plan to target a hit list of premium retailers. The first year went better than expected and they're already listed in Selfridges and Whole Foods. Meenesh said the volumes aren't huge but it's given the brand a launchpad to target larger retailers.

The name game

Coming up with an idea and carrying out research will get you thinking about what to name your business. If selling your knowledge, the company could be named after you – for example, 'Emma Jones Advisory Services'. In which case, job done! But if you're looking for something else, think of a name that:

- is easy to spell

- has an available domain name

- is not already registered with Companies House (use the free web-check service to access existing company names at **www.companieshouse.gov.uk**)

- people will remember.

You might want to protect the name with a trademark. See later for information on how to go about that.

Most domain registration websites offer alternative name suggestions when searching for domain availability, which can offer inspiration:

- 123-Reg | **www.123-reg.co.uk**

- GoDaddy | **www.godaddy.com**

- 1&1 | **www.1and1.co.uk**

If you get stuck, visit Enterprise Nation (**www.enterprisenation.com**) where you will find people who can help you: the site is buzzing with talented copywriters and wordsmiths.

SWOT analysis

With your idea, and now your research in-hand that supports it, prepare a SWOT analysis. This stands for: **S**trengths, **W**eaknesses, **O**pportunities, **T**hreats and looks as follows:

Strengths

What are my strengths?

What can I do better than anyone else?

What resources do I have?

What's my unique selling point?

Weaknesses

What are my weaknesses?

What should I avoid?

Where do I lack skills?

What might hinder my success?

Opportunities

What opportunities do I see?

Does my idea tap into any trends?

Are there any emerging technologies that could help my idea?

Has there been anything in the news related to my idea?

Threats

What threats might I face?

Who's my competition?

Does changing technology affect my idea?

3. Write a Plan

Abusiness plan will act as your map. It will guide the business from start to growth, with reference to milestones along the way.

The plan will include information about how you intend to get started and what your ultimate objectives are – and how you aim to get from one to the other. You might want to start a business and sell it in a few years' time, or grow to a point where you wouldn't want to grow anymore.

Of course, you'll need to refer to resources: what you have already, what you'll need and how you'll pay for it.

So, after coming up with an idea and doing your research, writing the business plan is your first practical step to starting your business. With it under your belt you can say, "I'm off!"

Or IMOFF. It's an easy way to remember the headings to include in your business plan: Idea, Market, Operations, Financials and Friends. Have these as headings in your plan and you've taken a big step closer to becoming your own boss.

Idea

What's your idea?

Market

Who will be your customers or clients? And who is your competition?

Operations

How will you develop the idea, promote it and provide good customer service?

Financials

Can you earn more than you spend, so that the business makes a profit? Do you need any funds to get started?

Friends

Do you have a support network on hand for when you need business advice? Are there complementary businesses you've identified with whom partnerships are a possibility?

> **REGULAR REVIEW:** *Return to your plan to check progress against targets or to make amends as you respond to new opportunities.*

A business plan section by section

Company ABC

Business Plan
20xx-20xx

[You could choose to do a 12-month plan, two years or up to five years.]

Contents

Executive Summary
The Idea
The Market
Operations
Financials
Friends & Family *[This title would be more like 'Advisory Board' if preparing the plan for a bank or funder.]*

Executive Summary

Summarise what's in the rest of the plan. Something like this:

The vision for ABC is to become the leading company for selling abc to xyz. This plan sets out how the vision will be achieved in the period 20xx-20xx. It outlines the product on offer, provides data on the market and shows how the company will be operating profitably within the first three months.

Having identified a clear gap in the market, I'm excited about the opportunity to start and build a successful business that will offer a quality product [or service] to a well-defined market.

A. Person
Founder, Company ABC

The Idea

Include here your 'elevator pitch'; what is your product and how will it benefit the customer?

This is the opportunity to explain the idea of the business in a few sentences.

The Market

Customers

Who will be your customers? Include the quantity, their demographic profile, geographic locations, social backgrounds; essentially any strong data that shows you know your audience.

Competition

Who is selling a similar product/service? How do you differ from them? What is your unique selling point?

You can do this by producing a table that lists the competition. Outline what makes you stand out in the market: is it that your service will be online, that you'll charge a different price, have an innovative marketing approach or offer the service with a special extra twist?

Operations

The CEO

You have come up with the idea for the business and you've done your research on the market. Now it's time for the reader to know a bit about you! Note your background, skills, experience and any credentials for running this business. Plus information on other key members of staff (if there are any).

Sourcing

If this applies to your business, refer to how you'll source your product/service. You may be making it yourself!

Sales & Marketing

How will you promote what you offer to your customers? Include a brief sales and marketing plan with headings like this:

Press – how many press releases do you plan to distribute each year and to which press channels: newspapers, magazines, radio, etc.?

Online – *will you have your own blog/website? Mention other sites that you'll approach for reciprocal links.*

Partners – *what about marketing tie-ups with other companies selling to the same audience?*

You know where your customers are, so let your marketing plan show that you'll reach them in print, online and even in the streets!

Systems

You've sourced the service/product and told customers about it. Refer here to the process customers will go through to buy from you and the systems you'll have in place to deliver in time and on budget. Systems that may include online ordering and payment, a professional call-handling service to take orders or maybe some specific software.

Friends & Family

In starting and growing your business, will you call on friends and family for advice? If so, refer to this here; mention your board of advisers, your experts-on-call, your support network!

[See 16. Support for details on how to access expert advisers and find a mentor whose details you can also include here.]

Financials

Last but not least come the figures. Make this as clear as possible and it's probably best to do it in table form:

	Year 1	**Year 2**
Revenue		
Overheads		
Office rent		
Salary		
Stock		
Technology		
Marketing		
Travel & expenses		
Projected profit		

Drawing up a simple financial forecast will highlight any need to borrow money.

4. Register the Company

When you set up in business, there are a couple of organisations you need to contact: Companies House and HM Revenue & Customs (HMRC). Before registering with either, have a think about the company status that suits you best.

Self-employed

This status means you are working for yourself. You keep records and accounts of your own activities and, in acting alone, get to keep all the profits – but are also solely liable for any debts.

Limited company

Limited companies exist in their own right, with the company's finances kept separate from the personal finances of its owners, so your liability is limited.

Partnership

If you'd like to be self-employed but want to work with a friend or colleague, consider a partnership. It means that two or more people share the risks, costs and workload.

Many of the companies featured in the following pages have formed a partnership. They all comment on how a mix of skills and experience is helping the business to grow.

IF YOU'RE UNSURE, ASK: *The status of your company will affect how much admin you have to do and the kind of financial records that you need to keep and file. Take advice from your accountant or local tax office on which one to choose. See later for details on how to access free consultations with qualified accountants.*

Being social

Should you decide to start a social enterprise – a business trading for social and environmental purposes – there are additional legal structures to consider, including:

- community interest company (CIC)
- industrial and provident society
- charitable status.

To find out more about launching a social enterprise or creating a CIC visit:

- Social Enterprise UK | **www.socialenterprise.org.uk**
- CIC Regulator | **www.cicregulator.gov.uk**
- 'Setting up a social enterprise' via GOV.UK | **www.gov.uk/set-up-a-social-enterprise**

Companies House

When registering with Companies House, there are three options from which to choose. You can buy a ready-made company from a company formation agent, incorporate a company yourself by sending documents and a registration fee to Companies House or register online via GOV.UK. If you decide to complete registration yourself, see form IN01 – application to register a company. It can be easier to go with a formation agent as they do the work on your behalf.

- **GOV.UK** | Incorporate via GOV.UK (**www.gov.uk/register-a-company-online**) and pay £15.

- **Self-incorporation** | Visit the new company registration page of the Companies House website: **www.gov.uk/limited-company-formation/register-your-company**. Complete form IN01. Post to Companies House with relevant fee. Standard service fee of £40 (documents processed in eight to ten days). Same-day service fee is £100.

- **Company formation agent** | Register with a formation agent such as Companies Made Simple (**www.companiesmadesimple.com**). Prices start at £16.99 for standard company registration.

HM Revenue & Customs

The rules on registering a new business with HM Revenue & Customs are pretty clear-cut. You are required to register as soon as you start earning from any business activity. As stated, you can choose to register as self-employed, as a partnership, or as a limited company. Each category has its own filing requirements, as we'll explore now.

Sole trader/self-employed

The calculation of tax and National Insurance owing is done through self-assessment. You either need to complete a form CWF1, or simply call the newly self-employed business helpline. It should be done by 5 October after the end of the tax year in which you started your business to avoid a fine.

- Form CWF1 | **www.hmrc.gov.uk/forms/cwf1.pdf**

- Helpline for the newly self-employed | 0845 915 4515

It's not onerous to complete the form and, once registered, you'll be classified as self-employed and sent a self-assessment tax return each year, which you complete, showing your income and expenses from self-employment as well as details of your employment elsewhere (if that applies).

You will be subject to tax and National Insurance on any profits you make, but the good news is that any losses incurred can be offset against your employed income (if you have any), which could even result in a tax rebate.

Deadlines

Self-assessment tax return deadlines are as follows:

- paper tax returns should be received by HMRC by 31 October

- online tax returns should be completed by 31 January (giving you an extra three months).

Useful links

- Leaflet SE1 – 'Thinking of working for yourself?' | **www.hmrc.gov.uk/leaflets/ se1.pdf**

- Helping you understand self assessment and your tax return, HMRC | **www. hmrc.gov.uk/sa**

Partnership

According to HMRC, a partnership is where:

> "Two or more people set up a business. Each partner is personally responsible for all the business debts, even if the debt was caused by another partner. As partners, each pays income tax on their share of the business profits through self-assessment, as well as National Insurance."

In terms of filing requirements, each partner should complete a partnership supplementary page as part of their individual self-assessment tax return. This is in addition to a partnership return, which has to be submitted by one nominated partner and show each partner's share of profits/losses.

Deadlines

The deadlines for partnership tax returns are as follows:

- paper tax returns should be received by HMRC by 31 October

- online tax returns should be completed by 31 January (giving you an extra three months).

Limited company

Limited companies exist in their own right, with the company's finances distinct from the personal finances of the owners. What this means is that the company is liable for any debts, not the individual owners, as is the case if you are self-employed or in a partnership.

In April 2008 it became legal to form and run a limited company with just one person, without the need to involve anyone else (prior to this you also needed a company secretary). As noted, you can form a new limited company by registering with Companies House via GOV.UK (**www.gov.uk/limited-company-formation**) or by using a company creation agent.

As well as registering with Companies House, you also need to let HMRC know you are operating as a limited company. And you will need to set up and register a PAYE scheme, as you are an employee of the company.

- Register PAYE scheme | **www.hmrc.gov.uk/newemployers**
- New employer's helpline | 0845 60 70 143

In terms of filing requirements, you should complete a self-assessment company tax return at the end of the accounting period. The return will show the company's taxable profits and whether any corporation tax is owed, and can be filed online at **www.hmrc.gov.uk/ct**.

The return should also be filed with Companies House to comply with the Companies Act 2006. This can be done free of charge, using the online WebFiling service at Companies House: **ewf.companieshouse.gov.uk**.

On your returns, you can claim an element of your expenses for working from home. You can also claim travelling expenses, subsistence and a proportion of your phone calls.

Deadlines

Whereas filing deadlines for self-assessment and partnership tax returns are specific dates, that is not the case with company tax returns, which must be filed 12 months after the end of your company's corporation tax accounting period.

IN GOOD ORDER: *Keep records of your business dealings – this will make it much easier to complete tax returns when the time comes. Keep hold of* **receipts** *of business-related* **purchases**; **copies of invoices** *to customers;* **bank statements**, *especially if you don't yet have a separate account for the business (it is worth starting one);* **utility bills** *(if you are starting the business from home and using part of the house for business), which can be claimed as a business expense and so reduce your tax bill.*

For advice from HMRC on good record keeping, visit: **www.hmrc.gov.uk/startingup/ keeprecs.htm.**

VAT

Whichever company status you choose, if your business turns over more than £85,000 (in the 2018/19 tax year), or you think your turnover will soon exceed this amount, you should also register for value added tax (VAT).

You can voluntarily register at any time. Being VAT-registered can bring credibility with certain customers, but adding VAT to your invoices may make you more expensive than competitors and you will have to file a VAT return four times a year.

- 'How and when to register for VAT', HMRC | **www.hmrc.gov.uk/vat/start/ register**

Accountant accompaniment

Talk to a qualified accountant about the structure that is best for your business. And consider employing their services to complete your tax returns. Even if your accounts are very simple, it is well worth seeking professional advice, particularly as the rules and regulations can change frequently and without warning.

You can access free consultations with accountants through the Enterprise Nation marketplace **www.enterprisenation.com**.

Useful links

- 'Starting a Business', HMRC | **www.hmrc.gov.uk/startingup**
- 'Tax Help – and advice for small business' | **www.businesslink.gov.uk/taxhelp**

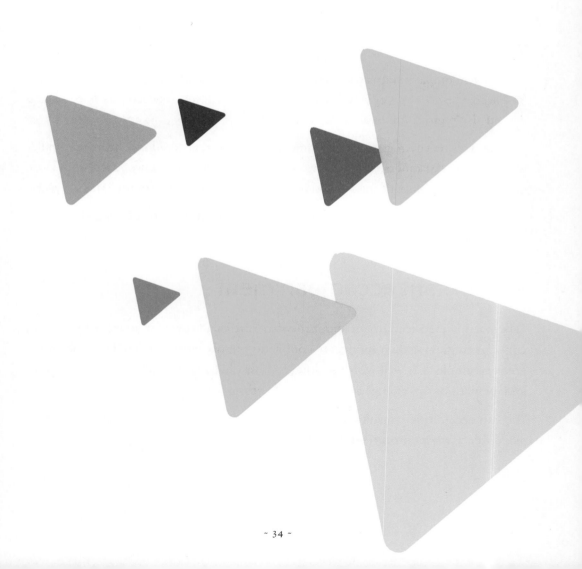

5. Protect the Brand

You have now registered with Companies House and HM Revenue & Customs. Your final consideration should be your intellectual property. You may decide to register a trademark to protect your company name or brand or, if you've come up with a unique invention, a patent. Registering either means that companies can't come along and use your name or invention without your permission.

The four forms of IP

There are four different kinds of intellectual property that you can protect:

1. **Patents:** These protect what makes things work. For example, says the Intellectual Property Office (IPO), "what makes a wheel turn or the chemical formula of your favourite fizzy drink".

2. **Trademarks:** These are "signs (like words and logos) that distinguish goods and services in the marketplace".

3. **Designs:** What a logo or product looks like: "from the shape of an aeroplane to a fashion item".

4. **Copyright:** An automatic right that comes into existence for anything written or recorded.

Register and protect your intellectual property by visiting the UK Intellectual Property Office website (**www.ipo.gov.uk**).

6. Take Care of Household Admin

When starting out, you'll likely be starting from home – your own, your parents' or maybe a friend's. It's the best way to start, keeping costs low and the commute short. In other words: more time and money for the business.

You'll probably be outsourcing work as opposed to employing staff, so there's no need for lots of people to come into the office each day. And you can meet clients and contacts in the local hotel or serviced work space. It's also good to know you're not alone in starting at home – over 70% of businesses do. You may have a few questions around household admin and who you need to tell. Here are the answers.

Q: Do I need planning permission?

A: You'll only need planning permission to base the business at home if you answer 'yes' to any of these questions:

- will your home no longer be used mainly as a private residence?
- will your business result in a marked rise in traffic or people calling?
- will your business involve any activities that are unusual in a residential area?
- will your business disturb the neighbours at unreasonable hours or create other forms of nuisance such as noise or smells?

If your house is pretty much going to remain a house, with your business quietly accommodated within it, then permission won't be required. If you're unsure, contact your local council to seek their views (**www.planningportal.gov.uk**).

Q: Do I need to tell the local authority I'm working from home?

A: Depends on whether you pass the planning test. If you need planning permission, you'll have to inform your local authority. If not, you won't! As a home-based business, you will be covered by small business rate relief so there's no requirement to pay rates on the part of the house you're using as an office unless the business forms part of a shop or you've converted part of the house into a business premises. Check out the GOV.UK guide to business rates at **www.gov.uk/introduction-to-business-rates/working-at-home**.

Q: Do I need to tell the landlord?

A: Yes, it's best to let them know that you will be working from home. Good news is, the government announced a model tenancy agreement in August 2014, making it much easier for people in social and private housing to use living space as work space. Since then we've seen some social landlords such as London & Quadrant (**www.lqgroup.org.uk**) organise business training for tenants. A welcome sight.

Q: What about my insurance provider? Do they need to know?

A: Yes, do inform your insurance company. Tell them about the equipment and stock you have at home. An upgrade from domestic to a business policy is not expensive so don't be put off in making this call. Your insurance provider is likely to recommend that you also take out public liability insurance in case anyone who comes to visit suffers an injury in or around your home office. See the next page for a guide to all kinds of insurance.

Q: Do I need protection for when customers and contacts come to visit?

A: Yes, carry out a health and safety check, which is easy to do by following the steps set out by the Health and Safety Executive (**www.hse.gov.uk**) in their *Homeworking* guide (available at **www.hse.gov.uk/pubns/indg226.pdf**).

Q: Should I tell the neighbours?

A: Yes. When working from home, it's worth keeping your neighbours firmly on side. You don't want them getting annoyed by any deliveries or distractions. If you know of a time when there'll be an unusual amount of activity in your home office, let them know in advance and perhaps send a bottle of wine or gift to compensate.

Insurance ins-and-outs

There are different categories of insurance which you need to know about to secure the policy that's right for you. The main ones are:

1. Professional indemnity – relevant to businesses offering services and knowledge. Provides protection if you receive a claim alleging a negligent act, error or omission committed by you in the course of the conduct of your professional business.

2. Public liability – advisable to have if clients are visiting your home office and/or you are supplying goods to consumers. This will protect you in the event of potential injury to business visitors and/or damages arising from the supply or sale of goods which have caused injury to a third party or their property.

3. Business interruption – covers your potential loss of revenue following a material damage loss.

4. Employer's liability – only applies when you have employees. Offers protection in the event of death or injury to them sustained in the course of their employment.

5. Motor insurance – this is different to standard car insurance, which does not include business use. If you have a vehicle dedicated for business, you should buy motor insurance or get a business extension on your car insurance policy when using your existing car for business travel.

6. Home insurance – you are likely to already have a home insurance policy but this will generally not cover business activities carried out at home or business equipment within the home. Speak to your insurance provider and upgrade to a business policy. This is not usually costly but it will ensure you're protected.

Creating the perfect work environment

Wherever you've chosen to set up shop, create the perfect work environment by following this quick checklist to ensure you're working profitably and productively.

Find dedicated space

Try to create an area at home that functions as your dedicated workspace. That way you can better adjust into business mode. It's also useful for making clear to friends and family that when you're in your home office, you're working.

This dedicated space could be a spare room, in the attic, under the stairs, or even the garden shed.

Invest in a good desk and chair

You could be spending a good few hours each day at the desk and in your chair, so be sure they're both sturdy and comfortable. Buy a chair that's designed for computer use – and try it out first. The back experts say your feet should be flat on the floor and your back straight.

When it comes to computers, the top of your monitor or laptop screen should be at eye level and about an arm's length away from you. There are all sorts of docks that can help with this, but there's also no harm in using a sturdy pile of books and an external mouse/keyboard to achieve the same end.

Have a vision

Put a vision board up on the wall and stick pictures on it that represent your personal and business ambitions: places you want to visit, targets for the company, and people you enjoy spending time with. Glance at it each day. Remind yourself of everything you're working for.

A SPRING CLEAN: *Wondering what to do with all the stuff in the room that you want to use as your home office? Rent storage with a company like Bizspace (**www.bizspace.co.uk**), Access Self Storage (**www.accessstorage.com**) or Big Yellow (**www.bigyellow.co.uk**) and have your goods accessible but out of the way, or give them to a recycling company so that your unwanted items can go to a home that does want them!*

Roam free

Install Wi-Fi so it's possible to work from anywhere on the property. To get started you need a wireless router. You may have received one free from your internet service provider. If not, check out respectable suppliers such as Netgear (**www.netgear.co.uk**). See *Getting connected* in the next chapter if you need support.

PETS AND PLANTS: *Having plants in your home office can reduce work-stress, experts say. Seeing a growth in greenery can also help you feel less alone, and it helps with humidity levels, dust and productivity. Likewise, pets are known to reduce stress and can be an excellent source of company!*

Support on tap

And finally, surround yourself with supporters. Friends or family, peers in online forums, contacts met at events; they can all help when it comes to celebrating your success or raising your spirits on a day that doesn't quite go as planned.

Leaving home

For those days when you'd rather work outside the four walls of the home office or if an external office is right for you from the start, find available space in enterprise hubs, co-working spaces and serviced offices. All needs and budgets catered for!

7. Your Tech Setup

Putting together a tech setup for your new business needn't mean starting from scratch or spending lots of money. Once your business starts to grow, you can upgrade your tech as and when money becomes available.

To start with, there are affordable and free solutions that can get you up and running in no time at all. Chances are, you have some of them already.

So, let's take a look at what you might already have and what you might need to buy. We'll separate them by hardware and software.

Hardware

Computer

When starting out, using a shared computer will be just fine. Bear in mind, however, that in the first few months of starting your business, you may find yourself working more hours than usual trying to put it all together. So let your friends and family know you may be hogging the computer!

Also, when your business starts to grow, the information you collect – info on your customers, clients and contacts; including financial details – will become more and more valuable. You might then start to think twice about sharing your computer with other people.

You may already have your own laptop. If you don't, when you've got a bit of money behind you, look into buying one for your new business. Budget laptops start at around £200, but when buying a computer it sometimes pays to buy the best you can afford in order to prepare for the future. Look out for these key features:

Processor

The processor is the speed of your computer. The higher the number, the faster your computer can run.

Memory

More memory (RAM) improves performance and enables your computer to run more programs at once. A common frustration amongst computer users is how long it can take to launch programs and switch between them. More RAM equals less waiting.

Hard drive

The hard drive gives you space for data and programs. This can easily be expanded with an additional, external, hard drive. You may be surprised at how quickly it will fill up, if your laptop is your only computer and you're also storing personal data, like music and photos, on it.

Peripherals

Multifunction printer

I think it's too early to pronounce the printer dead, especially if you use a multifunction printer. It's a real space-saver – imagine keeping a printer, scanner, photocopier and fax machine in one office.

External hard drive

External hard drives are great for adding more storage capacity to your computer but they're especially useful for backing up your machine. This is an important process, which you should do regularly – imagine what would happen if your computer crashed and wouldn't restart, or if it was dropped or stolen.

Macs have backing-up software built-in; as do the latest PCs. If not, try SuperDuper! for the Mac and True Image for the PC.

- SuperDuper! | **www.shirt-pocket.com/SuperDuper**
- True Image | **www.acronis.com**

Keyboard and mouse

If you're going to use a laptop, you probably won't get an additional keyboard and mouse. But you should think about it. Lots of time hunched over your laptop screen is no good for your neck and back. With an additional keyboard and mouse, and a stand that raises your laptop to eye-level, you can prevent a lifetime of aches and pains.

Some companies produce keyboards/mice which are ergonomically designed to prevent repetitive strain injury (RSI).

VoIP phones

You can make serious savings on your phone bill by using a VoIP phone. VoIP stands for 'voice over internet protocol' and basically means making calls over the internet rather than your phone line. As such, it's a much cheaper way of making calls (it's sometimes free). And it's the easiest way to set up a second line. Check out VoIP phones by a company called IPEVO.

- IPEVO | **www.ipevo.com**

Software

You may already be using many of these programs, so there's no need to splash out when setting up your business. Once it grows you can upgrade to more advanced versions if required. To start, here are the basics. Later we'll look at software (much of it free or very affordable) for when your business is up and running.

Office software

The industry standard in office software is Microsoft Office. If you're trying to save money, try these free alternatives:

- OpenOffice.org | **www.openoffice.org**

- Google Docs | **www.google.com/docs**

Both do pretty much everything that Microsoft Office does, and can open and save Microsoft Office files as well.

Web browser

Internet Explorer and Safari both do a good job when it comes to web browsing, as does Firefox. Also consider Google Chrome as it's faster, more secure and more customisable.

You can add features that will help you do your work and manage your lifestyle. These include features to control your music (without having to switch programs), comparison shop and even change the way your browser looks. It's a free, small download, and it works on Macs and PCs. Its speedy and uncluttered nature makes it particularly good for netbook use.

• Google Chrome | **www.google.com/chrome**

Email

If you've got Microsoft Office you might use Outlook, which includes calendar and address book features. On Macs, Mail is standard.

An alternative is provided by the people who make the Firefox browser. It's called Thunderbird and can do pretty much everything that Outlook can. You can also use it with web-based mail, like Gmail.

• Microsoft Office | **www.office.com**

• Gmail | **www.gmail.com**

• Thunderbird | **www.getthunderbird.com**

SIGNATURE TOUCH: *Make the most of the opportunity every time you click 'send' on an email. Include a professional email signature or sign-off that has your basic contact details (company name, website, postal address, telephone, etc.). And consider including a discreet mention of any seasonal or product offers, and your social media sites.*

Instant messaging and VoIP

Lots of instant messaging programs also allow you to make video and voice calls. Skype integrates text, voice and video chat. With it you can make free calls to other

Skype users and to landline or mobile phones for a small fee, deducted from pay-as-you-go style Skype credit.

You can assign a landline-esque phone number to your Skype account in order to receive calls at your computer, using a VoIP handset, or divert calls to your mobile when out and about.

- Skype | **www.skype.com**

On the move

Now that you've found the right technology for your office it's time to take it outside. If you ever get tired of your four walls, it's good to know that it's possible to work elsewhere. With a few simple tips and tricks you can enjoy total flexibility, and work from almost anywhere.

With your computer

If you have a laptop, you pretty much have all you need to work on the move. Almost all laptops come with built-in wireless receivers, so you can hop onto Wi-Fi in public places like coffee shops and libraries. But if you're not sure whether there'll be ample power supply where you're going, a spare battery is well worth considering.

Should I buy a tablet computer or a laptop?

Like the rest of the world, you've probably been tempted by gorgeous tablet computers like Apple's iPad. But should you buy one instead of a laptop? Can you really get as much business-work done on a tablet?

Well, it really depends on the nature of your business. If you'll be out and about a lot, visiting clients and customers, then buying a tablet becomes a serious consideration. But if your work will involve lots of sitting at a desk or writing long documents, you may find that a tablet PC is not for you. The iPad is constantly improving as a business machine thanks to the App Store, but be prepared to buy an external keyboard to cope with long writing sessions.

The future of computing could lie somewhere between tablets and laptops: ultrabooks. Ultrabooks are really thin, fast laptops. They have traditional features, like a full-size keyboard and trackpad, but usually no DVD drive and limited hard drive storage. That's okay, though, as a lot of your work will take place in the 'Cloud' (more on that later!). Because of their size and weight, ultrabooks are really portable.

Getting connected

You'll need broadband right from the start: during your research, while you're setting up your business, through to when it grows and takes over the world!

Your two main options are ADSL broadband, which is offered by companies like BT, Orange and Sky, and cable broadband from Virgin Media. The biggest difference is that ADSL requires a phone line, while cable broadband does not.

The advantage of cable broadband is that if you don't have a landline phone, and always use your mobile, you can save money by not having to pay line rental on your phone as well as on your internet connection. It's often faster, too, but you'll need to check whether it's available in your area. ADSL broadband is more commonplace and there are lots of companies offering it. As always, read the fine print before you sign anything. Here are some things to look out for:

Price

Some broadband prices seem really cheap but often the prices advertised are for the first few months of an 18-month contract, so make sure you know what you're getting into.

Usage

Some broadband companies will set restrictions on the amount of data you can download in a month and sometimes even charge you extra if you go over your agreed limit. These limits rarely affect most users, but if your business is the kind that needs to send and receive lots of information, look for deals with generous monthly download allowances. Or, better still, unlimited downloads.

Customer support

If you're installing broadband for the first time, you might need some help setting up and, once you're up and running, for what to do when your connection suddenly drops. For these sorts of queries it's handy to have good customer support, so check to see what's on offer and, crucially, how much it should cost to call for help.

Network

Setting up a network used to be the work of professionals and, I suppose, in big companies it still is. But setting one up for your home by yourself is much easier these days.

There are two types of wireless router: one for ADSL internet service providers, like Sky and BT, and another for cable internet, like Virgin Media. Check with your internet service provider to find out which is the best router for your type of connection.

If you didn't get a router from your provider, check out Netgear.

•   Netgear | **www.netgear.co.uk**

The Cloud

If you already use web mail, you'll be accustomed to the idea of your messages and contacts being available from any computer or device connected to the internet. So, how about running your entire business from any computer or device anywhere?

The Cloud refers to web apps. You run them through your web browser and all the data is stored online, so in effect you can use them from pretty much any computer anywhere!

The best example is provided by Google, whose Google Apps (**www.google.com/a**) offering includes email, instant messaging, a calendar, word processor, spreadsheet and presentation software, as well as a website builder. It's free and easy to use.

All the work you do is stored in 'The Cloud' so you can log in and out from anywhere and see the same information. Also, if your computer crashes or you buy a new system you won't lose any data or have to reinstall it on a new machine.

10 free cloud apps for your business

Cloud apps are not only fantastically useful, they don't take up room on your computer and you don't have to worry about backing up your data. They're also, more often than not, free to use.

Here are ten of our favourite free cloud apps for business.

1. Office 365 (**www.office365.com**) | This online productivity toolkit includes email, calendars, Skype for Business and Office productivity applications; everything you need to run your business in the cloud.

2. Dropbox (**www.dropbox.com**) | Dropbox is like a thumb drive in the sky. It's a folder that sits on your computer, but its contents are stored remotely and synced across other computers and devices that are signed into your Dropbox account. No-nonsense sharing, if you're working with others, and peace of mind that all your work is backed up.

3. Evernote (**www.evernote.com**) | Evernote is a bit like Dropbox, but for your brain. It helps you "remember everything" by allowing you to capture notes and ideas, photos and screen grabs, sounds and links, sync them automatically to the cloud and access them from practically anywhere – great for the planning stages of your business.

4. OneNote (**www.onenote.com**) | A digital notebook that synchronises your notes across PCs, Macs, tablets and smartphones. You can even access your notes on the web.

5. Google Docs (**docs.google.com**) | Google Docs includes apps for word processing, spreadsheets, presentations, drawings and forms – except all the apps run inside your browser rather than on your desktop. All of your work is stored in the cloud and it's easy to collaborate with others in real time on the same document.

6. Google Analytics (**www.google.com/analytics**) | When your website is up and running, you'll want to know how many people are visiting. Google Analytics is free, and helps you understand your website statistics, including where your visitors are from, which pages they visited the most, and how they found your website in the first place.

7. HootSuite (**www.hootsuite.com**) | If social media is part of your marketing plan – and it probably is! – there's no better way to manage your social media presence than with HootSuite. It keeps you on top of your Twitter, Facebook and LinkedIn accounts, as well as what your customers and potential customers are saying about your business.

8. Trello (**www.trello.com**) | There's so much to do when starting a business, but you can keep on top of all your tasks with Trello. This is like a Pinterest for tasks and ideas and can be shared with others.

9. Basecamp (**www.basecamp.com**) | If some tasks involve other people and form part of larger projects, check out project management software, Basecamp. It allows you to share files, deliver projects on time and keep communication organised and out of your inbox.

10. MailChimp (**www.mailchimp.com**) | To make sure your business message is in other people's inboxes, put together a newsletter with MailChimp, send it out to your customer mailing list and track its success. Just make sure people have signed up to your mailing list before hitting 'send'!

THE EASE OF FREE: *many cloud apps offer free trials so you can see which ones work for you without having to spend any money.*

8. Working 5 to 9

You don't need to give up your studies or throw in the day job to get all this done. Nor do you need to for the next two stages – launch and growth. You can plan the business, register the business and continue to run the business successfully by 'working 5 to 9' – this is the term I apply to the five-million-plus people in the UK who are working or studying by day, and building a business at night and weekends.

It's a sensible way to start and grow. If you're working a day job, you give yourself the time to build confidence and cash flow in the business, and can keep putting money aside until you're ready to go full time in your own venture.

Here's what you need to do regarding your current job and boss in order to make this as smooth as possible.

The contract

If you have written terms and conditions of employment they are likely to contain reference to the pursuit of personal business ventures outside your contracted working hours. The clauses to look out for include 'the employee's duties and obligations' and what is commonly known as 'whole time and effort'. These clauses require the employee to devote the whole of their time, attention and abilities to the business of the employer.

If your contract contains these or similar clauses, don't despair, as it doesn't necessarily mean you can't pursue your business. Many employment contracts are drafted using standard templates with little consideration to personal circumstance. You know your job better than anyone, so if you don't think your business venture will affect the way you do your job, it probably won't – and your employer will recognise this. Having checked how things stand in the contract, it's time to talk things through with your boss.

The conversation

Treat it as an amicable and informal conversation to gauge your employer's initial reaction. I asked Patrick Lockton, a qualified lawyer, for his take on the matter and advice on how employees should go about having this conversation:

> "When you approach your employer, be prepared to negotiate, be flexible and compromise. If you think it appropriate, make it clear your business venture will in no shape or form affect your ability to do your job or affect your employer's interests. If anything, it will make you a better, more confident and experienced employee and it will not cost your employer a thing."

Patrick goes on to say:

> "After having such a conversation, you can do one of two things:

> 1. if your employer has not expressed any concerns about your intentions and you have no concerns of your own, disclose your intentions to your employer anyway. Treat it as something you want to do for the sake of clarity and for the record, as opposed to something you want their permission for; or

> 2. if your employer has expressed concerns, try and negotiate a package that you are both happy with. Address their concerns, agree some ground rules and get their permission in writing. Give your employer as much helpful information as possible. If you are going to need some time off or to change your hours then this is the time to bring it up.

> Always take written notes so that you don't forget what was said and so you can remind your employer what was agreed."

So long as you're not competing with your employer or breaching their trust, you shouldn't have any problem at all in pursuing your 5 to 9 ambitions. After all, as Patrick says, your employer benefits from all the new skills you're picking up, and it doesn't cost them a penny in training or resources!

CASE STUDY

Name: **Nisha Katona MBE** | Business: **Mowgli Street Foods**

Nisha Katona is on a mission to protect the Bengali cuisine her Indian family cooks. The ex-barrister didn't want the recipes to be forgotten when the first generation of immigrants passed away and has built her passion into a national chain of restaurants.

"Mowgli is based on the way we eat at home. Very often vegan, always gluten free, quick and amazing flavours. I was teaching those recipes and my classes were always full. That's how I knew people wanted to cook this stuff. I actually think it's one of the easiest, smartest ways of eating – I call myself a curry evangelist."

She attempted to get a kiosk in high-profile shopping centre Liverpool ONE but they didn't see the potential.

"They didn't take me seriously because I wasn't a restauranteur. We didn't get the kiosk but it ended up being the best thing in the world.

"I ended up taking this small site that no one else wanted. It was down this little road that didn't really have anything else on apart from a tea shop. We opened to queues down the road that, thankfully, have never diminished."

Nisha said loneliness was one of the biggest challenges she faced starting a business.

"My family has been an amazing support, but you're still doing things by yourself. It's been the best thing though. The truth is that I don't feel I've worked a day in my life. Anything that's gone a little bit wrong just teaches you how to do it better next time."

Mowgli's brand and culture has been built around Nisha's personality.

"I design every building myself. I had a designer who wanted us to go with more of an ethnic style. But when you've been a self-employed barrister for 20 years, you've got a strong vision and you've got some confidence. I came into business with the same vision.

"I built my own culture and decided how I wanted to do things. I built something I call the maternal management model – I run Mowgli the same as how I run my family. Love flows through the business, especially from the top down".

Mowgli Street Foods just signed its fourteenth lease in five years. Nisha said female founders are highly underrated.

> "The world doesn't owe you a living. You've got to have a unique gift and skill that fills a unique gap in the market. If you're doing another job, keep doing it. Keep pushing at the other door, but if it doesn't open, then move on. Don't jeopardise your finances and career and your livelihood for something that won't work. Be humble about it. What you're selling might not be everyone's cup of tea, so look hard at your product and the feedback you're getting."

Nisha was awarded an MBE for services to the food industry as part of the 2019 New Years Honours.

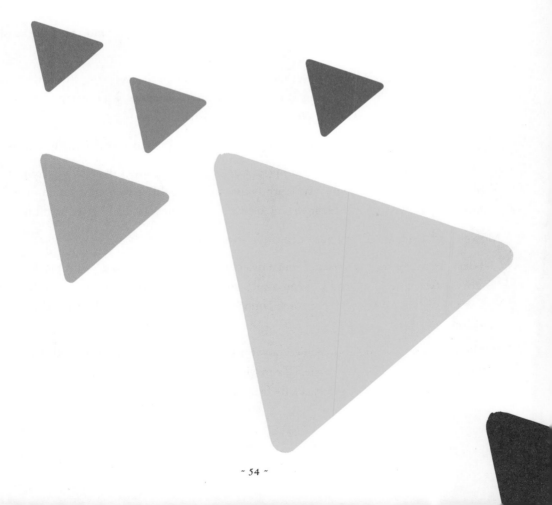

9. Starting on a Budget and Straightforward Finance

It has never been more straightforward to build a business on a shoestring of a budget and keep on top of finances with basic spreadsheets or software. You probably already have a computer and a mobile phone, so you might not need to buy much more equipment (depending on your business). Here are some tips for keeping costs low.

Start the business from home

Why take on the cost of an office when the spare room/attic/garden shed will do just as well? Think of the money you'll save: no premises, no commute, no overpriced sandwiches at lunchtime…!

Embrace social media

Make the most of free or low-cost technology tools to raise your profile and make sales. *12. Make Some Noise!* offers details of the major social media tools and how they can best be used to your benefit.

Beg, borrow and barter

When starting out, access all the free and discounted resources you can.

THE BEAUTY OF BARTER: *Many start-up businesses barter their goods and services, e.g. "I'll produce a sales brochure for you, in exchange for a handmade cushion for my living room." This works well – both parties get what they want. But take heed of the tax implications. Bartering means money doesn't show up in your accounts, but there has been an exchange of goods and services which implies a taxable activity. The taxman could view bartering as a way to avoid tax. Nevertheless, with so many beneficial arrangements underway, maybe it's time they revised the tax situation?*

Skills swapping is an approach that's worked well for marketer, Paula Hutchings:

"My first experience of skills-trading was in Sydney when I first set up Marketing Vision Consultancy. I wanted a website for my new business but I was short of funds so I didn't really want to pay for it! I was lucky enough to find a web designer who was willing to build the site for me in return for marketing support with a side business of his. This trade worked out really well. I went on to trade for graphic design work, photography and even hair-cuts! It helped me to get things I needed for the business when funds were tight, but it also helped me to gain valuable experience when I was just starting out. I still skills-trade now if the right opportunity arises. To me it is important to support small business and start-ups in the same way that people supported me when I first set up. It is also a great way to make new contacts."

Make the most of offers

One last tip for keeping costs low at the start: don't forget to join Enterprise Nation so you can benefit from offers and access deals from top brands.

These tips and techniques will help your budgeting. When it comes to getting hold of funds, there are a number of places to look.

Funding

Friends and family

Friends and family are people you can trust – and asking them for money hopefully won't come with strings attached. Do consider having a written agreement, though, that covers the amount borrowed and a payback schedule.

Start Up Loans

Introduced by the government in 2012, Start Up Loans are made to entrepreneurs across the UK. Alongside a loan, you also receive a mentor who offers help throughout your business journey.

Crowdfunding

Crowdfunding is fast becoming a popular route to secure start-up and follow-on funding. It involves sourcing funds from a crowd of others and there are three main types of it:

1. Reward

This is where people fund your business (or product) in exchange for rewards. Possibly the most well-known site to offer this form of funding is Crowdfunder (**www.crowdfunder.co.uk**) and there's also the US version of Kickstarter (**www.kickstarter.com**).

2. Equity

This is where people invest in your business in exchange for equity, i.e. a percentage of the business.

3. Loan

This is where you raise a loan and repay with interest.

In raising funds from the crowd, not only do you secure the capital you need, you can also attract attention and an audience of potential customers. As crowd funding has become more popular, the number of crowdfunding platforms has increased.

Top crowdfunding platforms

Crowdcube | **Crowdcube.com**

Crowdfunder | **Crowdfunder.co.uk**

Crowd2fund | **www.crowd2fund.com**

Funding Circle | **www.fundingcircle.com**

Indiegogo.com | **www.indiegogo.com**

Kickstarter.com | **www.kickstarter.com**

Seedrs.com | **www.seeedrs.com**

Spacehive.com | **www.Spacehive.com**

Unbound.co.uk | **www.unbound.co.uk**

The bank

Ask to speak to a small business adviser at your local bank. Take a copy of your business plan with you and be prepared to talk it through.

> **A CLEAR DIVISION:** *Open a bank account early on so you don't mix up your business and personal finances, which may complicate record keeping.*

Investors

Angel investors and venture capitalists can help raise large amounts of start-up funding or development capital for businesses looking to grow. It might be an idea to consider this route further down the line. It doesn't have to be a gruesome experience (à la *Dragons' Den*), though, as there are plenty of funds and investors out there who are eager to part with their money and back good ideas. What's more, the government has made it financially attractive for angels to invest through the Seed Enterprise Investment Scheme (SEIS) which offers individual income tax relief of 50% and exemption from capital gains tax (CGT) on any proceeds of sale of a SEIS investment.

Visit the dedicated SEIS website (**www.seis.co.uk**) for details and the Business Finance For You site (**www.businessfinanceforyou.co.uk**), which offers a listing of available grants and funds, searchable by your local area.

In the words of an Angel

Andy Yates is an experienced angel investor and serial entrepreneur. In terms of what he looks for, he says:

> "Great businesses are created by great people. I always look out for the three Ps – passion, personality and perseverance. I also back entrepreneurs who really listen and learn. The ability to be flexible, take on board advice and feedback and adapt a product or service to win customers is the real key to unlocking success."

- Angels Den | **www.angelsden.co.uk**
- Funding Circle | **www.fundingcircle.com**
- Find Invest Grow | **www.findinvestgrow.com**
- Angel Investment Network | **www.angelinvestmentnetwork.co.uk**
- UK Business Angels Association | **www.ukbusinessangelsassociation.org.uk**

See later for details on accelerator programmes that will take your business from start to growth at speed, and often come attached with funding.

Straightforward finance

When planning a business you'll want to be sure earnings are higher than outgoings. Earnings are also referred to as revenue, turnover or income and this should be a greater figure than outgoings, overheads or costs. Let's look at the items that come within each category.

Incoming

Earn from selling your product or service and any associated income opportunities. For example, you set up a business selling unique handmade cushions. From the outset, earn income from:

- Selling 24 x handmade cushions at £25 per cushion = £600 income per week

- Speaking at events to teach others how to make cushions = £150 per event

- Custom requests, e.g. a unique and one-off production = £75 per item

- Developing a blog on the topic of cushions that attracts cushion-istas as readers and paying advertisers as your customers = £priceless!

Outgoings

Here are the costs; some payable at start-up stage and others ongoing:

- **Salary** – how much do you need to pay yourself? (You will be pleasantly surprised at how thriftily you can live when not commuting.)

- **Property** – start the business from home and avoid the cost of a pricey office.

- **Raw materials and equipment** – what are the materials you need to deliver and promote your finished cushions? And do you need any equipment to make that product; a sewing machine, computer, printer, smartphone or camera?

- **Insurance** – be insured from the start and choose a policy that covers all your needs.

- **Website/promotion materials** – we will cover in Chapters 10–12 how you can build a home on the web and promote the business on a shoestring of a budget.

Keep records of 'Incoming' and 'Outgoing' in a basic Excel spreadsheet or accounting software as in the following. See later for an example invoice and how to keep a record of invoices raised and amounts paid.

INCOMING	
Product sales	£xx
Sponsorship/Advertising	£xx
Other contracts	£xx
OUTGOINGS	
Salary	(£xx)
IT	(£xx)
Office	(£xx)
Raw materials/equipment	(£xx)
Insurance	(£xx)
Marketing & promotion	(£xx)
Other	(£xx)
PROFIT	£XX

 **PART II. Launch**

You have your idea. It's supported by research and a plan pointing you in the right direction. You've sorted out all the technology you need to get going. And with the company registered, it's time to get into business by making sales and some noise.

10. Create a First Impression

You may have started out by making sales to friends and family who know and trust you to deliver. To attract new customers, it's important to create the right first impression, whether that customer meets you at an event or visits your home on the web. Here's guidance to getting it right and offering a professional welcome.

Your home on the web

You have the tools and connection to get online. The first thing to do is build a presence through a blog, website or store. Not only is a website your window to the world and home on the web, it has become an essential requirement for any new business. Your site can be used as a powerful marketing tool and a way to make money. Having the right technology and knowledge allows you to build, develop and maintain your site. And you can do it all in-house.

Let's look at the three main ways to develop a professional-looking online presence.

1. Blogging

Blogging is a website or part of a website that's regularly updated by an individual or a group of bloggers. There are blogs on any number of topics and the fact that anyone can start blogging for free makes the medium diverse and exciting.

It's an easy way to get online, as you write posts on your topic of choice, upload images and video, and become the go-to place for customers looking for your advice/

tips/services/products. Search engines love blogs and the more you write, the higher up the search-engine ranks you will go. Writing regularly is likely to lead to a loyal readership and it's an effective way to communicate your news with existing and potential customers. Readers can add their comments to your entries if you allow them, and you can use your blog to answer questions and establish yourself as an expert in your field.

It's free and easy to get blogging:

- Blogger | **www.blogger.com**
- Typepad | **www.typepad.com**
- WordPress | **www.wordpress.com**

See 11. Make Sales *for details on how to make money from your blog.*

Now you see me

After getting to grips with blogging, why not try your hand at vlogging? This stands for video blogging and is an effective way to interact with customers who want to see you, your products and other happy customers. Vlogging expert, Niamh Guckian, offers tips on how to vlog like a pro:

Vlog how-to

"Vlogging can help you tell people your story: a demonstration of your skills, an atmosphere piece, or an interview.

The gear: Become an expert on your chosen camera, whether a phone or something fancier.

Where possible use manual control with your camera – this applies to white balance, exposure and focus. Learn the rules and then have fun breaking them.

Use focus and depth of field to add style to your shooting. Using a tripod sets your work apart from amateur shooting and allows for good steady shot composition.

Safety: Using a small camera can make you feel like you can take risks that you wouldn't otherwise. This has advantages at times but don't take unnecessary risks. Don't shoot from rooftops or get into water!

Light: As a video-blogger, you will mostly be working with available or natural light. Try to get the most from what's available at the time.

Sound: Audio recording is a specialist art form. What we need to achieve as self-shooters is clean and non-distorted sound. Distorted audio is not fixable, and can usually be prevented.

Interviews: If your piece is interview-based, engage with the contributor, communicate with them and let them know clearly what you want them to do. Create an atmosphere where the contributor is comfortable, and make sure they know they can stop and start again, or ask questions.

Make sure the interview is a sequence, that it has a beginning, middle and end, and can stand alone if necessary.

Export and upload: Learn about the optimum settings and platforms for your finished piece."

2. Your own website

Build your own website that you can spec to your own requirements or invest in a template website. Let's look at both options.

DIY

You have decided to build your own site or have a developer take care of it for you.

The first thing to do is buy a domain. A domain makes up a part of your website and email address. So, for example, the domain name I own is enterprisenation.com. My website address is **www.enterprisenation.com** and my email address is **emma@ enterprisenation.com**. Both use the enterprisenation.com domain name.

A domain isn't only your address on the web, it's also a big part of your brand, so think carefully when choosing one. There are domain registration companies whose websites allow you to check for available domain names and often suggest available alternatives.

Registering a domain name doesn't give you a website, just an address for it (and an email address). Think of it like reserving a car parking space. You've got the space, now you need to buy the car!

A hosting company will sort you out with the web space to host your site. This is measured in megabytes and gigabytes, just like the information on your computer.

In terms of how much web space you will need, basic hosting packages offer about 250 MB of space, but anything over 1 or 2 GB is more sensible and will also allow you to handle more traffic as your website grows more popular.

With a domain name and web space, potential customers should be able to type your website address into their browser and find out all about your business – just as soon as you've built your site. Finding a hosting company shouldn't be hard. Most domain registration companies, including those mentioned above, offer web space as a package; and hosting companies usually offer domain registration, too.

When it comes to hiring a designer, have a think about what you'd like your website to do for your business. The easiest way to start is to think of your website as a brochure, but remember to include the following pages at the very least.

Pages to include

- About us: the story behind your business and its mission.

- News: the latest and greatest of your products, business developments, maybe a topical focus if relevant to your business.

- Products or services: punchy with the detail, using images of your best work, and text and video testimonials from satisfied customers.

- FAQs: questions which you get asked. A lot.

- Contact us: email and social media details.

Choose a designer who has carried out work you like the look of and for companies in a similar kind of sector to your own. That way, the designer will understand what site you're after – and what your kind of visitor will be looking for, as well as how they like to browse and buy.

Brief a web designer/developer

Here's Emily Hewett's (**www.birdsontheblog.co.uk**) advice on how best to brief a web designer/developer:

"**Who are you?** Give a short summary of who you are and what you do. This will help the designer tune in to your particular sector. You'll also need to tell them about your market and how you fit into the larger scheme of things – e.g. competitors, local and national.

What do you want to achieve? For example: data capture, sales generation, footfall increase, etc.?

Who are you talking to? Outline a profile of your customer. Who are you targeting? Break it down in terms of sex, age, average income and location.

What tone are you using? Deciding on how you speak to your audience is important. You may be writing the copy yourself or you may have a copywriter to do this for you. In this section of the brief tell the designer if it's a laid-back chatty tone or formal. The tone of the copy needs to be reflected in the design.

What are your likes and dislikes? Provide examples wherever possible. It might be a certain colour palette or illustration style or it could be a format. Any of these things help the designer understand what you're looking for.

Are there any mandatory elements? Fonts, colours, logos, legal text, images, etc. This way they can make sure they produce something on-brand, adhering to your corporate image.

What's your budget? A good designer won't take a large budget and fit a job to it. They should find the most cost-effective way of producing exactly what you want. But if you have a small budget, the designer will have to make decisions based on that.

When do you want it? Make sure the deadline is clear.

Have you covered everything? Show the brief to a colleague or friend to see if they understand it. Once happy, send or talk it through with your designer and invite questions so they are aware you are approachable and that you are both working from the same list of requirements."

Template sites and payment systems

If DIY feels and sounds too much like hard work, there are a number of companies offering template websites that come with domain registration, hosting, e-commerce and a basic level of design as part of the package – over the page there's a comprehensive list of template site providers offering websites that can be set up today and trading tomorrow. Many e-commerce platform sites come with an in-built payment system; here are the main ones:

PayPal

PayPal has more than 100 million active registered accounts and is available in 190 markets, meaning you can successfully trade in all these markets!

The company offers three main products: website payments standard, website payments pro and express checkout. To enable your customers to buy multiple items, use a free PayPal shopping cart. To put the 'Add to Cart' button on your website you simply copy and paste the HTML code from PayPal to the coding of your own site (**www.paypal.com/uk/webapps/mpp/merchant**). Your customers then click the button to make a purchase. With PayPal, there are no set-up charges, monthly fees or cancellation charges, and fee levels vary depending on the volume of sales.

Stripe

Accept payments from major international debit and credit cards with Stripe (**www.stripe.com**), which charges 1.4% + 20p per successful charge, or less based on volume. Anything you earn via your website is transferred to your bank account on a daily basis. Setting up a Stripe account takes only moments, allowing you to start trading with immediate effect.

- Actinic | **www.actinic.co.uk**

- Big Cartel | **www.bigcartel.com** US-based Big Cartel has a focus on providing online stores for clothing designers, record labels, jewellers and crafters.

- Create | **www.create.net** Set up your site in minutes and benefit from email support plus online forums.

- Moonfruit | **www.moonfruit.com** Moonfruit Shopbuilder automatically creates a store on Facebook and a mobile version of your site.

- osCommerce | **www.oscommerce.com** An open source solution.

- Shopify | **www.shopify.co.uk**

- Squarespace | **www.squarespace.com**

- SupaDupa | **supadupa.me**

- Weebly | **weebly.com** Manage your site on the go via the Weebly app.

- Wix | **www.wix.com** Hundreds of designs to choose from and a drag-and-drop system to get you started.

Make your website legally compliant

These tips are offered by Joanna Tall, founder of **www.OfftoseemyLawyer.com:**

1. Display terms of use

"Think of your website like a board game you are about to play with your visitors. They arrive and are ready to play and you need to state the rules or else it will be chaos! So, for example, state what they can and cannot do – e.g. may they copy your materials? May they link to you? May they rely on the information you provide without double-checking with you or elsewhere? What liability are you prepared to accept? Provide a link to your terms of use, ideally on every page of your website or under a 'Legals' section.

2. Display your privacy policy

Most websites collect personal data on their visitors either by getting them to register on the site or sign up for a newsletter. By law you must tell visitors what you will be doing with this data and the best way to do this is to set out the information in a privacy policy. Again, a link to it on every page is best. More complex rules apply if you plan to collect sensitive information or information from children, or want to pass the information to third parties; for this you should consult a lawyer. Additionally, you are likely to need to register as a data processor under the Data Protection Act. Simply go to **www.ico.gov.uk** for more information.

3. If selling goods or services online, display your terms of sale

Just as with the board game example, you need rules for selling your goods or services. Most importantly, you need to get your visitors to acknowledge that they accept them. So ideally get them to tick a box stating that they accept them before they proceed to check out. You also need to draw their attention to their rights under the Distance Selling Regulations, e.g. cancellation rights amongst others.

4. Protect your copyright in the website content

Although you automatically own the copyright in the content that you create, best practice is to remind your visitors! Say, for example: "Copyright 20xx Lawyers R Great Ltd". And if your logo or name is trademarked, broadcast the fact! After all, you will have spent money in getting it that far and it will enhance your brand in the market.

5. State who you are!

By law you need to state a full postal address and contact number and if you are a limited company, the company's registered address, number and country of registration. This also applies to your emails."

Distance Selling Regulations

One thing to bear in mind when selling goods or services to consumers via the internet, mail order or by phone, is compliance with the Consumer Protection (Distance Selling) Regulations 2000. The key features of the regulations are:

- You must offer consumers clear information including details of the goods or services offered, delivery arrangements and payment, the supplier's details and the consumer's cancellation rights before he or she buys (known as prior information). This information should be provided in writing.

- The consumer has a period of seven working days from delivery of the items to cancel their contract with you.

These regulations only apply when selling to consumers, as opposed to businesses. In the event of a contract being ceased, you have to refund money, including delivery charges, within 30 days of the date of cancellation.

3. A presence on other sites

Maybe you'd prefer to start raising your profile and making sales via other established platform sites, as opposed to your own. Whether selling homemade crafts or business concepts, there are a number of options.

The upside is that these sites attract customers on your behalf, and some of them attract customers from all over the world. Here are seven sales platforms that enable you to sell:

Alibaba

Having a presence on this site enables you to buy and sell with, and source supplies from, companies across the globe. The site has visitors from 240 countries and regions, with over 1 million registered users in the UK. Through the site you can locate suppliers or make sales of your finished product direct to customers. Alibaba is a champion of international trade; carrying out research on the topic, providing a platform for traders to interact, and promoting overseas sales as a form of business that is wholly viable, regardless of company size.

- **www.alibaba.com | @AlibabaTalk_UK**

Amazon Marketplace

You may be used to buying from Amazon, but have you considered the site as a platform from which to sell? Have your products appear before millions of customers all around the world by signing up to Amazon Marketplace. It offers two sales options: a package for casual sellers who expect to sell less than 35 items a month (a fixed fee per sale plus a referral fee), and, for more seasoned sellers, there is the 'sell a lot' package, which has a monthly charge plus a referral fee for unlimited sales that do not have to be in the Amazon catalogue.

- **www.amazon.co.uk/marketplace**

eBay

Having a store on eBay means you are opened up to an international audience and a lot of potential customers.

- **www.eBay.co.uk**

eBay expertise

*Dan Wilson (***www.wilsondan.co.uk***), an eBay author, offers five tips on how to make the most of the mega marketplace:*

1. Start small

"Go slow until you've found your way. Start with a few, easy-to-post items and learn about eBay before boosting your range and prices. Don't stake too much on your first eBay bet.

2. Sell like you mean it

The eBay marketplace is competitive and you'll lose out unless you have top-notch listings. Craft fabulous item titles, make impeccable pictures and write descriptions that tempt buyers. Be truthful and honest and look professional from the start.

3. Be quick off the mark

Buyers have come to expect great service. Dispatch orders quickly — preferably within 24 hours of payment — and well packed, and make sure you reply to emails and other communications swiftly, too. The quality and speed of your replies and dispatches has an impact on customer feedback.

The StartUp Kit

4. Put a lid on postal costs

Understand postage and packaging costs and make sure you factor it in to your costs where necessary.

5. Loyalty means profit

When you're building your eBay business, encouraging repeat buyers is important. Once a buyer trusts you as an online seller, they're likely to keep coming back. Offer discounts and incentives with every dispatch and cross-market complementary products."

Etsy

With its tag line 'Your place to buy and sell all things handmade' this is still the mother of all craft sites. Since the company launched in June 2005, more than 500,000 sellers from around the world have opened up Etsy shops and buyers of Etsy-listed products span more than 150 countries.

For anyone who makes handmade items, the power of this global platform cannot be denied.

- **www.etsy.com** | **@etsy**

Facebook

With more than 1 billion users across the globe and 30 million in the UK, a significant number of your present and potential customers spend time on Facebook every single day. If your business isn't there, it's missing out. Countless small business owners in the UK use Facebook to quickly and cost-effectively grow their company. The easiest way to start is through having an effective Facebook Page.

- **www.facebook.com**

iTunes

If you are a creator of audiobooks, a publisher of podcasts or developer of apps, then the iTunes platform is your route to market. For apps, Apple gives 70% of revenues to the seller. Over 60 billion apps have been downloaded from its App Store, making it the world's largest mobile application platform. Become a registered Apple developer for the iPhone (**developer.apple.com/iphone**), submit audio books to iTunes via Audible.com (**www.audible.com**) and create iBooks for the iPad through the iBookstore. Apple is opening up a world of opportunity for content creators and app developers.

- **www.apple.com/itunes**

Enterprise Nation Marketplace

Small business network, Enterprise Nation has its own marketplace to match small businesses with talented professionals and advisers. If you're a supplier of advice on sales and marketing, making the most of digital technologies, access to finance etc., create a profile and be matched with small business owners looking for the advice you offer. Over 13,000 advisers now use the marketplace as their route to market.

- **www.enterprisenation.com**

> **A TOP-QUALITY IMAGE:** *Whether you decide to start online with a blog or a full e-commerce site, place high-quality images on your site and printed materials so that on first click or at first glance, a customer is inclined to buy. Take professional images yourself or consider subscribing to a stock image library such as* **www.istockphoto.com**. *Other image libraries include:* **www.imagesource.com**, **www.photos.com** *and* **www.gettyimages.com**. *Search for Creative Commons licensed images you can use commercially from Flickr at* **www.compfight.com**.

Rise up the search engine ranks

Promote your business and website through search engine optimisation. Commonly referred to as SEO, this is the process by which you can improve rankings for your website in the top search engines such as Google, so that your site appears on the first few pages of results rather than on page 75.

Google is a search engine that uses software known as 'spiders' to crawl the web on a regular basis and find sites to add to their index. There are steps you can take to make it easier for the spiders to find and add your site.

> **THINK LIKE A BUYER:** *When thinking of the keywords to use in PPC (pay per click) ad campaigns (and in search engine optimisation) think of the words your buyers will be using when searching for your product or service. Use the Google AdWords Keyword Tool to find out the most popular search terms. Apply these words in the campaign and include them in the text on your site.*

Start with the homepage

Provide high-quality, text-based content on your pages – especially your homepage. If your homepage has useful information and good quality, relevant text, it's more likely to be picked up by the spiders. Beyond the homepage, write pages that clearly describe your topic/service/product. Think about the words users would type to find your pages and include them on the site.

Make contributions

Identify influential bloggers and sites in your trade/industry, contact them and offer to write posts. You can also improve your visibility by writing helpful comments in forums and on other people's posts.

Be well-connected

Improve the rank of your site by increasing the number of other high-quality sites that link to your pages; these are referred to as inbound links. For example, if you're running a competition, go to sites that promote competitions and add yours.

Register your site with the major search engines.

- Google | **www.google.co.uk/addurl**
- Yahoo! | **search.yahoo.com/info/submit**
- Bing | **www.bing.com/webmaster/submitsitepage.aspx**

> **SEARCH ENGINES LOVE LINKS:** *Another way to increase your ranking in the search results is to link to other sites and vice versa, but think quality here as opposed to quantity. Sites offering the best 'link juice' are trusted domains, such as news sites, and very popular sites. You could post comments on such sites and blogs and include a link back to your site. Try these handy hints: approach sites complementary to your own and suggest reciprocal links; ensure that your website link is included in all your social media profiles; register with the major search engines (see above); add your domain to local search services such as Google Maps, Qype, Yahoo! Local and BView.*

- **www.google.co.uk/maps**
- **www.yelp.co.uk**
- **www.uk.local.yahoo.com**

Tagging

A webpage's title, referred to as a 'title tag', is part of the SEO mix and can make a difference to your search rankings. It is also the text that appears in the top of the browser window. Include in your title tag the main key phrase you'd like the search engines to associate with your webpage and keep it to 60-90 characters in length. Duncan Green of Moo Marketing is an SEO expert and explains: "the title tag on the homepage for Moo Marketing reads: 'Moo Marketing – Search Engine Marketing – PPC Management – Search Engine Optimisation'. As you can see the title element is 85 characters long, contains three key phrases and identifies the subject of the webpage."

Pay per click advertising

The results from your efforts in SEO will appear on the main engines as a natural or 'organic' search result. But have you spotted results on the right of the page when searching for items yourself? These are paid-for results and referred to as pay per click or PPC advertising. PPC is where you pay to have ads displayed when people type in certain words, in the hope it will attract more visitors to your site.

Google AdWords is a form of PPC advertising. Think of the key words or phrases you reckon your customers will be searching for and apply them in your Google campaign. Link to your homepage or other pages on the site where you're running a promotion and make the most of geotargeting, which lets you target your ads to specific territories and languages. You are in full control of the budget and campaign duration.

* **adwords.google.co.uk**

Spread the word

Make it easy for visitors to spread word of your site through social sharing. Have your site Tweeted, Pinned and Liked and make the most of this viral effect. You can add these social bookmarking tools by visiting AddThis (**www.addthis.com**) and choosing the icons you'd like to have displayed on your site.

Your business in print

Print is far from dead, so get yourself some business cards, postcards and promotion flyers to hand out at business events, social occasions, and to just about anyone you meet! Have fun with designing your cards at **www.moo.com** and get a range of designs printed in each batch. Sell vintage fashion? Upload pictures of your products to the reverse of each card. Offer web design services? Have a portfolio of sites you've designed there.

Look at my logo!

When you contact potential customers you'll want them to read about you and get a sense of your style. You can do this very effectively with a nice-looking logo or company design that's repeated across all your promotion materials, from business cards to brochures.

Think about what you'd like as your company font, colours and layout. Have a go at designing this yourself or hire the services of a designer/neighbour/friend. Good presentation can make a world of difference. This may just be the difference you need to clinch a contract.

Find a professional to design your logo via these sites:

*   Enterprise Nation Marketplace | **www.enterprisenation.com**
*   CrowdSPRING | **www.crowdspring.com**
*   Fiverr | **www.fiverr.com**

Office address

If you are running the business from home there are a couple of reasons why you might not want to put the home address on your business card: it might sound too domestic, and you might not want people turning up on your doorstep!

You can solve this with a P.O. Box number, which is easily set up with Royal Mail (**www.royalmail.com/pobox**). Alternatively, you could invest in a virtual office, which gives you a more tailored and personal service than a P.O. Box – plus you get a nice-sounding address and a place to use for meetings. Having a virtual office enables you to choose the address that suits you best, have post delivered to that location, and then forwarded on to you. Companies providing this service include:

*   Regus | **www.regus.co.uk**
*   Bizspace | **www.bizspace.co.uk**
*   Bruntwood | **www.bruntwood.co.uk**

When holding meetings, consider hiring professional meeting space. Many offer serviced addresses and secretarial services too, so there could be great continuity for your clients if they only have to remember one address.

On the phone

When running the business from home, consider who will be picking up the phone! It's cheap and sometimes free to get an 0845 local rate number or an 0870 national rate number for your business. This will hide where you're based and divert your calls to wherever you specify. But beware: sometimes having such a number – especially with national rates – might put customers off ringing you.

If you use a landline number it's best to have a separate line for your home and your business. These days you don't need to invest in an actual second line. You can use a VoIP (voice over internet protocol) phone, which uses a broadband internet connection to make and receive calls, something we looked at earlier.

*   Skype | **www.skype.com**

Another idea is to get some help from a call-handling service. They will answer your calls with your company name, text urgent messages to you and email the others, giving you a big business feel for about £50 per month. Services on offer include:

*   Moneypenny | **www.moneypenny.co.uk**

*   MyRuby | **www.myruby.co.uk**

*   Answer | **www.answer.co.uk**

You might consider a 'follow-me number' to ensure you're available when you need to be and able to deliver the right impression to clients. A follow-me number involves choosing a number and directing calls from it to your landline or mobile. The beauty of choosing a number is that you have the option to select either a freephone or a geographical number so, say you'd like to have a Manchester area code, simply buy a number starting with 0161. The same goes for hundreds of other locations.

Offer virtual phone numbers where the caller pays a local rate, regardless of where you are, through Vonage (**www.vonage.co.uk**) or direct calls to you from a chosen number using internet technology and a virtual receptionist at eReceptionist (**www.ereceptionist.co.uk**).

In person

You are about to attend your first networking event or trade show and want to create a good first impression. With an attractive business card in hand, directing prospective customers to a good-looking online presence, all you have to do is follow the rules of effective networking!

The art of networking

- Wear your name tag (if you have one) on your right side. It's easy to catch sight of when you are shaking hands.

- Deliver a nice firm handshake and make eye contact.

- Say your name clearly and, in under ten seconds, tell the other person who you are and what you do.

- Listen carefully. Ask the other person plenty of questions about their line of business, their hobbies, etc.

- Be positive and energetic.

- Swap business cards.

- Send a thank-you email after the event, confirming any actions you and they have promised.

- Keep in regular and meaningful contact.

See 12. Make Some Noise! *for information on how to host your own event or attend a trade show to promote your business.*

A MEMORABLE EXCHANGE: *Richard Moross, founder of* **moo.com***, says: "The point of having a business card is to make a connection, create a relationship and leave something with the recipient that reminds them of you. Have cards that tell a story. Use that card as a sales tool, for sure, but also show appreciation by having cards relating to your customer." Richard achieves this by having images on his cards showing places he's visited and meals he's eaten. With 70% of* **moo.com***'s business being outside the UK, Richard travels a lot and the cards act as the ice-breaker in meetings as he tells the story behind the pictures.*

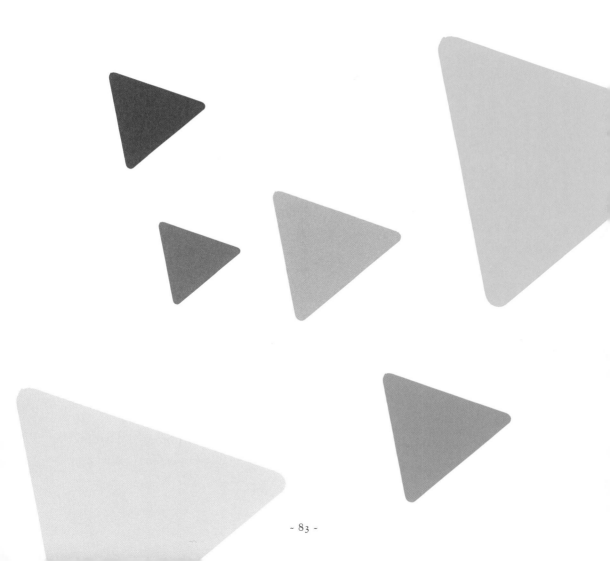

11. Make Sales

With a professional image established, you are ready to start making sales. This chapter will help you achieve that first sale, plus provide tips on how to make money from your website or blog.

1. Make a list (check it twice)

Draw on your existing resources, grab your address book and select the friends, family, colleagues and acquaintances you think might be interested in your product or service. Add to the list with details of local people and businesses, too.

2. Pitch up

Contact the people on your list and announce your new business venture. Consider this an opportunity to make your pitch, but don't be too pushy. Remember to address each recipient personally. No one likes a group email!

3. Follow up

Follow up in a few days time, either with another email or, better still, a phone call. Take some soundings as to the success of your pitch and react accordingly. If the potential customer or client sounds keen, go for it! Arrange to meet him or her to show your product or explain more about your service.

4. Meet up

Arrange a time and place to meet that's convenient for your potential customer or client. Be professional, but also likeable. These are equally important characteristics when making a sale.

If the customer agrees the deal, bring the meeting to a fairly speedy end. Your job is done – for now. It's time to head home and deliver on the promise you made with your first customer.

5. Make some noise

Once you've made your first sale – shout about it! If your new customer or client agrees, include them in a press release or write about them on your website or blog, so other potential customers or clients can see that you're well and truly in business!

> **SALES ARE FLYING HIGH:** *Have promotional flyers made to take to events or deliver through doors. Increase chances of turning flyers into firm sales by:*

- having a design that is memorable, possibly quirky and, ideally, that your potential customers will want to keep on their desk/in their bag/atop the kitchen shelf

- making the offer clear and confirming the benefits of buying

- including a call to action, i.e. a way in which the interested customer can contact you.

Warm up for a cold call

*Sales and marketing pro Jackie Wade (****www.winningsales.co.uk****) offers tips on how to make winning calls to customers...*

"**Ready:** Preparation and focus is key. Start with a call list and clear objectives; which business or household and who specifically are you calling (decision maker)? Are you clear on your message? What benefits do you offer?

Steady: Feel confident, think positive. What's the worst thing that can happen? They may say no... so what! Not everyone out there will want you, but someone will! Tone is more important than words so feel and sound confident and positive.

Go: Be natural, be you. Have a good opening 'hook' to grab attention – something interesting, new or different and make it relevant to the person you're calling. Avoid rambling – focus on a two-way conversation, not a fixed script. Develop a list of open questions which will allow you to engage with the person at the other end of the line, e.g. what do you currently do, how does it work, what might you like to improve? Listen for opportunities. Engage!

Grow: Agree action and follow up promptly or agree a call back, if no interest for now. A NO today may be a YES tomorrow; tenacity counts. Things change.

Remember, smile and then dial. Your aim is to spread the word about you and your business."

When making a sales call, do so standing up and smiling. To the person on the other end, you will come across as positive and confident.

Someone who certainly knows how to hustle is Rebecca Linnell of the Country Dog Hotel.

CASE STUDY

Name: **Rebecca Linnell** | Business: **Country Dog Hotel**

Rebecca Linnell told the kennel owners she volunteered for to get in touch if they ever wanted to sell the business. She was working with strays in Thailand when they called with the news that they were ready to hand over the reins and her partner's parents bought the business.

In-spite of working there, she would never board her own dogs. The desire to create a kennel that met her own high standards provided the inspiration for the Country Dog Hotel, but it was splitting up with her partner that gave Rebecca the push to launch her own business.

"I was on my own with my two biological children and two foster children. I was a stay-at-home mum and a single mum and I thought; 'what can I do where I'm available for the kids and that I'll love?'. I wanted to be a really positive role model."

Rebecca hasn't spent any money on advertising beyond a handful of boosted posts on Facebook and Instagram. In the beginning, she just listed the business on a Facebook page and other buying and selling sites.

"We started to get customers trickling in. Then it started to go crazy. I was replying to more people to say 'no' than people to say 'yes'. We couldn't keep up with it. I thought we needed to put our prices up.

We never used to have time for marketing. We used to do it at midnight or one o'clock in the morning. We'd run the business during the day, sort the kids out, finish off with the dogs and then sit and do marketing stuff. Now it's easier because we've taken on staff."

She hasn't done a lot of PR, but was persistent about targeting *Country Living* magazine.

"I phoned them to find out who to contact and build rapport, so I wasn't just one of many. I hounded the journalist a little bit, but only a little bit!

I didn't hear anything for months and then I was walking into Glastonbury Festival when I got the call. They wrote a feature. A photographer came down and it ended up being a five or six page spread."

The obsession with the quality of the care has led to the Country Dog Hotel's five star rating on Facebook and 4.8 on Google.

"If I was going to do it, I wanted it to be the best. I'm quite passionate about that. It has to be the best in the country. That was from day dot. I'm quite persistent about that. I didn't want it to be run of the mill. We'll strive to make sure we are the best."

Rebecca advises people that are starting a business to get out of their comfort zone.

"I didn't have a lot of confidence. With what happened on a personal level it knocked my confidence big time. I could just wallow in it or brush myself off and think 'bugger this I'm going to do something great'. It was all about mindset."

The Country Dog Hotel's about to purchase a cottage at the end of the lane that will house smaller dogs. There's a plan to convert the summer house on the property into a spa that uses natural products and offers dog yoga too.

Selling into physical stores

Maybe you've started by selling products direct to customers at shows and fairs, but what about making sales via local shops?

Before you approach any shops, make a list of appropriate places where you think your product could work well. For example, does your town have gift shops or an art gallery, are there lots of boutiques that stock a range of different items? Think outside the box. Could your local coffee shop stock some of your items?

Five top tips for market placement

Laura Rigney is the author of Pitching Products for Small Business *and offers five top tips for pitching your product effectively:*

1. Be confident with pricing

"Selling in wholesale is a whole new ballpark as far as pricing is concerned. Make your product attractive to buyers with your pricing. A great way to show you're trying to help retailers is to set up a structured pricing system, i.e. 100 units or less £xx per unit, 101-500 units £xx per unit and 501 units or more £xx per unit. This system could also encourage shops and buyers to place larger orders.

2. Understand your product inside out

This means technical data as well as knowing why someone would buy it. When you get a meeting with a buyer or approach a shop owner, talk with confidence about where the product is made, by who, and using what kind of materials. Remember there is pressure on large retailers to "go green", so the more you can offer that as a potential supplier the more attractive you will be.

3. Be prepared

If a buyer places an order, how quickly will you have manufacturing, distribution and storage in place? Buyers won't expect a new small business to have a giant factory sitting waiting for someone to press the 'go' button but they will want a realistic estimate of how long it will be until your product is in their warehouses/on the shop shelf. Once you have given your timings, stick to them. Even if this means exaggerating the time it will take for them to be delivered. Better to be early rather than late!

4. Pitch perfect

If you're pitching in person, make it informative, exciting and interesting and where possible have evidence of past sales and customer satisfaction. You need to know your figures without having to look through paperwork and be prepared to haggle a little on prices. If someone likes your product enough and you have sold it well enough they will buy it, even if it's a few pennies more than they would like to pay. In the other direction, sometimes it may be worth offering a larger than normal discount as a trial for a first order.

5. Stay listed

When a company takes on your product it's called being listed. Once you are listed the work is just beginning! It is now time to stay listed for as long as possible and the way to do this is through marketing and PR. The more you promote your product and the shops/galleries/boutiques that are selling them, the more they will be bought by consumers thus encouraging buyers to place more orders with you!"

Lucy Woodhouse and business partner Meriel successfully pitched their frozen-yoghurt lollies to Sainsbury's as part of StartUp Britain's PitchUp competition. As a result, their lollies launched exclusively with Sainsbury's. Lucy says the secret to their success was:

- "a genuinely new product"

- "identifying our target audience"

- "really knowing the market"

- "being very aware of food trends and incorporating them into the products so we were ahead of the game, newsworthy and desirable"

- "a passionate pitch that didn't use Powerpoint".

PopUps

Want to hone retail skills, meet customers face to face and make sales? Why not try a high street PopUp and test new markets in the flesh?

Enterprise Nation launched the Clicks and Mortar campaign in June 2019 to give new British brands an opportunity to get onto the high street and fill empty shops with small business activity. A first Clicks and Mortar store opened in Manchester and, 4 shops later, the project has welcomed hundreds of start-ups and small businesses that trade in the shop for a week or fortnight before moving on to allow new businesses to move in.

The PopUp tenants are all online businesses that don't normally have the budget to take on a shop single-handedly and full time. Clicks and Mortar brings tenants together to share the cost and workload.

The project removes the friction for small businesses to test new products and sell on the High Street.

www.enterprisenation.com/clicksandmortar

The art of the pop

Here's how to ensure your PopUp experience is a profitable one.

- Place – choose a shop in a location that suits your products and is populated with people who represent your target market.

- Offer – ahead of moving into the shop, prepare sufficient stock at a price that's right for the particular area. Present the produce in a way that will attract customers' attention. Consider your own presentation and body language when approaching and dealing with customers.

- Promote – now you're in the shop, tell people you're there! Promote your presence to existing customers through social media. To attract new trade, consider partnerships with neighbouring retailers, flyers in the train station, releases to the local press and PopUp parties, lock-ins, cook-offs and fashion shows, to deliver a retail experience that customers will never forget!

Get the POP right and you'll see sales and profile on the UP!

Mechelle Clark made the decision that her business should be physical from the start and she's now loving life on the High Street...

CASE STUDY

Name: **Mechelle Clark** | Business: **Melt Aberdeen**

After being made redundant twice in the same year from the oil and gas industry and attending up to 60 job interviews, Mechelle realised that she had to create a job for herself and was determined it would be something she was passionate about. Driven by her love of cooking and good food, she set up Melt Aberdeen, Aberdeen's first made-to-order grilled cheese sandwich shop.

With the help of a £20,000 loan to fund everything from buying kitchen equipment to start-up costs, she founded her business, which has been trading for two years, serving up different toasties filled with quality local ingredients throughout the day. The business now generates a healthy turnover and Mechelle is looking to open further stores in Edinburgh.

Make money from your website

As traffic to your blog increases, so does your chance of generating income. Make a profit from your posts with this top-ten list of options.

1. Display advertising

Offer advertising on your site. The more niche your audience, the more likely you are to attract advertisers.

The information you'll need to provide includes:

* number of unique visitors
* number of impressions

- average duration of visit

- visitor demographics.

Write a basic rate card (see a few pages' time), add it to your site and send it to corporate marketing departments and media-buying agencies.

2. Google AdSense

This tool from Google does the work for you by placing relevant ads on your site and earning you money when people click on them. You can customise the appearance of the ads so they sit well with the style of your site.

- **www.google.co.uk/adsense**

3. Text Link Ads

These ads offer direct click-throughs from text on your site. You submit your site to Text Link Ads and then upload the ad code provided. It's your choice whether you approve or deny the supplied ads. Once that's done, you start making money as visitors click on the ads. Try this and Skimlinks, which converts words on your site to affiliate links so that you earn from those, too.

- **www.text-link-ads.com**

- **www.skimlinks.com**

4. Sponsored conversations

Get paid for posts (and now tweets) with services like IZEA that match bloggers with advertisers. Some doubt the ethical stance of paying a blogger to write something about a product but there's no doubt that it's a money maker.

- **www.izea.com**

5. Affiliate schemes

Sign up to affiliate schemes like the Amazon Associates Programme, where you can earn up to 10% in referrals by advertising Amazon products. The programme works by driving traffic to **Amazon.co.uk** through specially formatted links. You earn referral fees on sales generated through those links. Monthly cheques are sent to you from Amazon and it's easy and free to join.

- **affiliate-program.amazon.co.uk**

6. Sponsored features

This could include a host of options. Approach advertisers with suggestions of a sponsored eBook, e-news, podcast, webchat, poll or survey. These applications can be added to your site at a low cost yet generate good revenue.

For:

- eBook creation, try **www.blurb.com**

- a survey or poll feature, try **www.surveymonkey.com**

- email marketing, try **www.mailchimp.com**

7. Expert help

Offer your expertise and charge people to log on and watch or listen. This could be made available through teleclasses where you invite customers and contacts onto a call where you offer your expertise on a one-to-many basis, or an email training course using email programs such as Mailchimp (**www.mailchimp.com**) or Constant Contact (**www.constantcontact.co.uk**), or deliver a presentation to potentially thousands of paying customers via **www.gotowebinar.co.uk**.

8. Deals with suppliers

Do deals with suppliers. Hosting a travel blog? Agree a percentage each time a booking is made via your site. Hosting a wedding blog? Create a directory of wedding suppliers such as venues, photographers, dressmakers and caterers with an enhanced listing for those who pay.

9. Turn a blog into a book

Follow the lead of Alex Johnson who turned his Shedworking blog (**www.shedworking.co.uk**) into a book – and then a second book – which are now selling across the UK and overseas, acting as an effective marketing tool for the site!

10. Please donate

If you'd rather just ask for a small donation from your visitors, this is possible too via a donate feature from PayPal. Add a PayPal donate button to your site: **www.paypal. com/us/webapps/mpp/get-started/donate-button.**

* * *

Maybe you've decided to start selling products through your site. But if you only carry content, you'll need to add an e-commerce feature to make sales.

> **JUST-IN-TIME PAYMENT:** *Add a PayPal payment button to your site and you'll be able to accept payment from all major credit and debit cards, as well as bank accounts around the world. You can set it up in less than 15 minutes.*

Add an e-commerce plug-in

Want to open your site up to sales? Do so by plugging in an e-commerce tool such as:

- WordPress e-Commerce shopping cart – "suitable for selling your products, services, or fees online": **wordpress.org/plugins/wp-e-commerce**
- PayPal Shortcodes – insert PayPal buttons in your posts or pages using a Shortcode: **wordpress.org/plugins/wp-paypal-shortcodes**
- View a complete list of WordPress e-commerce plugins: **wordpress.org/plugins/ tags/ecommerce**

Add a shopping cart to your site

Make it easy for your visitors to click and buy. Check out these shopping cart providers:

- GroovyCart | **www.groovycart.co.uk**
- RomanCart | **www.romancart.com**
- CubeCart | **www.cubecart.com**
- Zen Cart | **www.zen-cart.com**

- ekmPowershop | **www.ekmpowershop.com**

- osCommerce | **www.oscommerce.com**

Research the product that suits you best, taking into account hosting provision, back-end admin, and built-in search engine optimisation.

SHOW ME YOUR RATES! *The purpose of a media rate card is to show potential advertisers what your site can deliver to them in terms of traffic and sales. To do this, include some key points:*

- A brief description of the site: What it does and for whom.

- Visitor demographics: Do you have data on the age of your visitors, their home region, gender, etc? If so, include it, as it helps build a picture of your audience.

- Site traffic: What are your unique visitor numbers and length of time spent on the site? Make a note if the figures are increasing.

- Costings: Do you have a cost-per-click (CPC) or cost-per-impression (CPM) rate? If so, include it here, along with the price of other sponsorship options. Offer a menu but leave some flexibility, with 'costed on a project basis' for sponsor features that would benefit from a more tailored proposal.

- Screen shots: Showing how and where adverts or sponsored features appear on the site.

- Media activity: Note where you've recently been covered in the media, online and off, so that potential sponsors can see how and where you're promoting the site.

- Testimonials: Positive comments from existing sponsors gives you credibility and gives confidence to the next potential sponsor.

- Team details: Who are the faces behind the site and what are their credentials? In other words, your background career and activities, etc.

Round this off with your contact details so that interested potential sponsors can get in touch and place an order!

12. Make Some Noise!

Sales are coming in, customers are happy and you want to tell the world about you and your new business. Profile brings new customers and new sales. Get yourself known in the press and online by making friends with the media, hosting events, entering awards and embracing social media.

Here's what to do.

Plot the script

Imagine yourself as the star of your own Hollywood movie. Are you an action hero, battling against the odds (think James Dyson) or a brand leading lady (think Mary Portas)? Plot the action and write the script. It will help you define your message to the media.

Find the right contacts

Research the journalists you think are interested in your field. Note their email addresses from the bottom of their articles, follow them on Twitter, get to know them and send them exclusive stories about you and your business.

> **LINK REQUEST:** *If you're being featured online ask the journalist if they can include a live link to your site. That way, readers can be on your site with one click.*

Write a release

Writing a press release costs nothing but your time, yet it can generate thousands of pounds' worth of publicity. If you're emailing a press release to journalists, write the text in the body of the email and include it in an attachment, too.

Your press release should have an attention-grabbing headline, the main facts in the first sentence, and evidence and quotes from as high-profile people and companies as possible in the main body of the text. Include great quality images wherever you can to lift the piece and put a face to the brand.

You could also use a press-release distribution service such as Journolink (**www.journolink.com**) to get your news in front of the right people. Access an offer on the service via Enterprise Nation.

If you don't get a response, follow up!

> **AN IMAGE SPEAKS LOUDER THAN WORDS:** *When a picture speaks a thousand words you can afford to talk less! Consider hiring a professional photographer to take pictures of you and your work. Maybe you can do this as a barter deal? Or pick up your own digital camera and do it yourself. Consider approaching a local college to suggest a photography student takes your images in exchange for including the end result in their portfolio. A journalist is much more likely to cover your story if you have great imagery to go with it. Use the images on your website and in promotion materials, and let your business speak for itself.*

Example press release: what to include

1. Attention-grabbing headline, followed by bulletpoint summary of whole story.

2. The first line is punchy and explains the what, who, why and where of the headline.

3. Back up the headline and intro with more detail – facts and figures if you have them.

4. Include a quote from you (or your business partner, if relevant).

5. Can you include a quote from someone else? A happy customer, industry expert or celebrity?

6. End with a call to action. Where can people go to find out more/how to download the report/which site to visit to claim a free gift, etc.?

7. Include 'Notes to Editors', with brief details on you and your company.

8. Remember to include contact details – your email address and telephone number.

9. Attach a relevant and interesting image.

Example press release: in action

[1] *GROWTH VOUCHER MARKETPLACE GOES TO SMALL BUSINESS NETWORK*

- *Small business network wins competitive pitch to deliver Growth Vouchers*
- *£30m of vouchers for small business to spend on accredited business advice*
- *Enterprise Nation's winning proposal gathers private sector funding to build, oversee and administer voucher scheme advice*

[2] *A small business network has announced it has been selected to deliver the Government's £30m Growth Voucher marketplace. Enterprise Nation won the competitive pitch with its proposal to use only private sector funding to build, market and administer the vouchers marketplace, which will connect small businesses with accredited business experts.*

[3] *The single platform will offer strategic advisers in finance, marketing, PR, general business and planning with the expertise to help small businesses grow. The vouchers will provide a Government-funded contribution towards the cost of advice for selected businesses.*

The typical value allocated to a small business will be £2,000.

[4] *Emma Jones MBE, founder of Enterprise Nation said: "This is an exciting initiative which could help accelerate the growth of thousands of small businesses at a critical stage of development - helping them to build long-term sustainability.*

"At the moment, access to business advice is sporadic and unregulated with no means available to understand the outcomes.

By bringing together accredited business advisers with the entrepreneurs that want to access good advice, we think the marketplace has the potential to deliver a significant boost to economic growth."

[5] *In his report 'Growing Your Business', the Prime Minister's Enterprise Adviser Lord Young said firms who "seek and engage external business advice are more likely to grow. But much more needs to be done to encourage firms to invest in their capability."*

The Growth Vouchers scheme will be launched early next year and vouchers will be available for 15 months. The delivery of the vouchers will be part of a random-testing exercise to help the Government gain a better understanding of the effect of business advice on growth and the wider economic implications of Government intervention.

Enterprise Nation has a community of over 100,000 small and start-up businesses. It delivers a comprehensive package of advice for entrepreneurs including an online support platform and lively in-person courses and events across the UK.

The scheme comes in the context of record numbers of start-up businesses across the UK, with more than half a million new registered companies each year for the past three years.

[6] *To register interest, please visit* **www.enterprisenation.com**

[7] *ABOUT ENTERPRISE NATION: Enterprise Nation is the UK's most active small business network. Its aim is to help people turn their good ideas into great businesses – through expert advice, events, and a modern membership. Enterprise Nation was founded in 2005 by Emma Jones MBE .*

[8] *For media enquiries, please contact Lizzie Slee (01234) 567890 liz@enterprisenation.com*

[9]

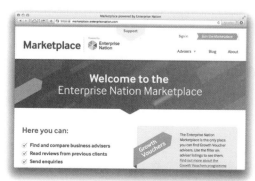

Tweet, Tweet

Follow media channels, journalists and personalities on Twitter so you're the first to pick up the news and media requests. Search the hashtag #journorequest to respond to journalists looking for stories like yours.

FREE PR CONSULTATION: *Join Enterprise Nation and benefit from free PR consultations with media experts on the platform.*

Kick-starting with PR

Greg Simpson, founder and director of Press for Attention PR (**www.pressforattention. com**) *gives his top 12 tips for building a successful PR campaign:*

1. Have a 'cunning plan'

"Too many people rush into PR and marketing campaigns with no real plan. You need to consider:

- What are the goals of the campaign?

- How do you want to come across in terms of tone?

- Key messages – what do you want to get across?

2. Consider how other companies get their messages across

What tactics can you use? PR stunts, press releases, controversy, photo opportunities, comment/opinion pieces, debates, flash mobs, press trips, celebrity endorsements, competitions. There are so many ways to get noticed. Blend them to your requirements and skills.

3. Research your customer/audience

There is little point getting a full article page in *Dog Grooming Monthly* if you sell organic ice cream to boutique hotels! Find out who your ideal customer is and research what they read, listen to and watch. Then, really take the time to read these publications and get to know what sort of stories they publish.

4. Find the news hook

Be honest, is your story really news? Examples include: new products, new staff, new promotions, new premises, anniversaries, company expansion, financial milestones and charity efforts.

You can also provide topical comment on a newsworthy subject. Keep an eye out for issues that affect your business or your customers. This takes practice and you need to establish credibility in your subject area first. Consider starting a blog that provides regular, lively and informed comment in your area of expertise to build your profile. I use WordPress (**www.wordpress.org**), which is free.

5. Got a story?

Got a story? Great! Now you need a simple press release for a journalist to refer to. People worry that their efforts don't sound flashy enough to warrant attention. But you aren't aiming for a Booker Prize. You're aiming for coherent and interesting news.

Use 'who, what, when, how and why?' as a framework and imagine yourself as the journalist. Is this definitely of interest to their readers? Is it simple enough to understand? Does it stand up on its own?

I would stick to a maximum of 300 words and keep the press release focused on the news angle.

6. Hit them between the eyes

Journalists get hundreds of press releases every day. Ensure that the headline and first paragraph sum up the entire story in a nutshell. Ideally, your press release should still make sense even if an editor dropped two or three paragraphs.

I call the journalist beforehand to outline my story. This helps iron out any creases and demonstrates that you are trying to work with them and their audience.

7. Don't be tempted to start hassling

I very rarely 'chase' a journalist once I have sent a press release. If it is good enough, they will use it. Hassling will not push it to the top of the pile and may see it heading towards the recycle bin. Be patient and able to help if the journalist does come back and don't go on holiday the day after you have sent a story out!

8. Think in pictures

Consider what makes you read a story when you flick through a newspaper. Headlines play their part but the impact of an interesting picture is greater still. People 'sell' stories, so ensure that anyone in your shot is clearly visible and captioned. Try to show the impact of the news – product shots are okay, but a product in the hands of a customer is better.

9. Build a relationship

PR is not a 'them v us' war with journalists. It's a working relationship, where both parties stand to gain. They get news/insight and you get free publicity in exchange for a fresh take on things or for your role in illustrating the impact of an issue.

10. Measure and evaluate

How do you know if your gym regime and new diet is working? You get on the scales (peeking between your fingers). Are you getting through to the right journalists? How many stories are you sending out? How many are getting coverage? How much coverage do they get? Do your pictures and even your key messages get included? Are you being invited to comment on topical issues?

11. Put your PR hat on and execute the plan

I know many small businesses that freeze when it comes to actually putting their plans into action. Schedule and commit some time every week to do something that contributes to your PR campaign.

12. A final tip

PR agencies spend vast amounts on media monitoring software for mentions of their clients or to keep in touch with specific debates. You can do a lot of it for free. Have a play with Google Alerts (**www.google.com/alerts**)."

Enter awards

Enter awards and competitions and enjoy the press coverage that goes with it. Many award schemes are free to enter and are targeted at young start-up businesses. Writing the entry will help to clarify your goals and vision, and winning will bring profile and prizes. To find out about upcoming awards across the UK, follow Enterprise Nation as we blog and tweet about the best of them!

Here are some to get you started:

- Shell LiveWIRE Grand Ideas Awards (**www.shell-livewire.org/awards**) – monthly awards for anyone aged 16 to 30 looking to get an idea off the ground.

- The Pitch (**www.thepitchuk.com**) – enter regional heats and pitch to experienced judges for a place in the national finals. Takes place across the UK.

- Social Enterprise Awards (**www.socialenterprise.org.uk/events**) – celebrates social enterprises of all ages.

- Female StartUp of the Year Award (**www.enterprisenation.com/survey/female-start-up-of-the-year-2019/**) – shining a spotlight on a female entrepreneur excelling in their industry.

- Next Generation Awards (**www.enterprisenation.com/nextgeneration/**)

Razan Al-Sous has seen at first hand the benefit of entering and winning Awards.

CASE STUDY

Name: **Razan Al-Sous** | Business: **Dama Cheese**

Razan Al-Sous decided to set up her own business making halloumi cheese, after fleeing war-torn Syria with her husband and three children in 2012. Arriving in Yorkshire, Razan struggled to find work, despite having a degree in pharmacology. She soon noticed how the halloumi cheese sold in the UK was of poor quality and only available seasonally, so she decided to start producing halloumi cheese using Yorkshire-sourced milk instead.

Using a £2,500 Start Up Loan, she bought the necessary equipment and her cheese became award winning within four months. Her business – Yorkshire Dama Cheese – now has a turnover of six figures, with products sold at Morrisons as well as online. It has also won a number of awards, including the World Cheese Award Gold Prize 2016, as well as being nominated by former Prime Minister David Cameron for recognition on International Women's Day 2015.

Host an event

Invite the press to come and meet you. This doesn't have to be an expensive affair; the secret is partnering with others who could benefit from being in front of your audience. Approach a venue and ask if you can host at no cost, in exchange for the venue receiving profile. Do the same with caterers. Then give invited guests a reason to attend – have a theme, an interesting speaker, a launch announcement, something that will grab their attention and encourage them to attend.

Make use of free online services such as Eventbrite (**www.eventbrite.com**) or Meetup (**www.meetup.com**) to send out invites and receive RSVPs.

Enterprise Nation members can upload events to the platform so they can be seen by thousands of small businesses each month and promoted via social channels.

Successful events in 5 steps – by Eventbrite

1. Planning = winning

Plan your event so you don't forget anything important. When will the event be held? When do you need to find a venue? When will tickets go on sale? When will you find sponsors by? When do you need materials delivered?

2. Take it online

Create an event page on Eventbrite so you can manage sign ups and communicate with attendees in one place. You can create custom URLs, promo codes and even different ticket types, such as an early bird rate.

3. Partner up

Start-ups grow and thrive off the back of collaborations. Put your event idea to contacts in the same space or at a similar stage and make it a group effort.

4. Get people talking

Be remarkable! Get creative and find a USP – an unusual venue, theme or format – so people remember your event. Once that's sorted, make the most of Eventbrite's social media integration to share your event... everywhere! And don't forget to create a Twitter hashtag so attendees can spread the word for you. #Bonus!

5. Stay in touch

The event doesn't end when guests leave. Write follow-up emails, newsletters, tweets, or connect on LinkedIn, and thank guests for attending. Encourage them to stay in touch and add them to your email list so they are in the loop about your next great event!

Attend events

Be seen and heard by getting out and about – a lot!

There's a wealth of events for start-ups. Most are free or low cost and offer an opportunity to learn from experts, mix with peers, and find new customers and suppliers

Enterprise Nation hosts a whole range of events throughout the year designed to help you start and grow. We'd love to see you at some of them! They range from one day class start-up workshops to local meet-ups plus training on the topics that matter to you most.

There's also...

- Global Entrepreneurship Week (November each year) | **www.gew.org.uk**
- NACUE events at universities and colleges | **nacue.com**
- StartUp Weekend: hosted in locations across the UK | **www.startupweekend.org**
- The Business StartUp Show | **www.bstartup.com**

Victoria Bustard's idea for a business came to her whilst attending an event. She hasn't looked back since.

CASE STUDY

Name: **Victoria Bustard** | Business: **Plant & Play Wildlife Centre**

Victoria has a passion for making children aware of the world around them and where their food comes from. It was this passion that encouraged her to set up the Plant and Play Wildlife Centre after studying zoology at university. The idea came to her when she was running a horticulture training programme for adults and noticed how little people knew about the outdoor world. This inspired her to set up a Saturday club for children to teach young people about nature from an early age.

With the help of a £5k Start Up Loan, she turned an old waste ground into an indoor play area and school allotment and opened the centre. Very quickly she was inundated with bookings and the classes have become so popular that she turned the centre into a roadshow available for school visits and birthday parties to ensure more children had access to the facilities.

Join a society, group or club

Signing up to an enterprise society, a local business club or network is good for business (and your social life). Check out these national business and society networks to find your natural fit:

- Enterprise Nation – a friendly community of business owners who benefit from daily content with members receiving profile, meet-ups, consultations with advisers, online masterclasses and a voice to government. **www.enterprisenation.com**
- 4Networking – national network of business breakfast groups. **www.4networking.biz**
- NACUE – the national organisation that supports and represents student-led enterprise societies and young entrepreneurs in universities and colleges across the UK. **www.nacue.com**
- IPSE – if contracting is the life for you, check out the free resources and events hosted by PCG. **www.ipse.co.uk**
- Virgin Media Pioneers – create a profile and connect with others, plus have the opportunity to pitch to Sir Richard Branson himself via this vibrant network of young entrepreneurs. **www.virginmediapioneers.com**

Attend trade shows

Promote your brand by attending the shows your customers attend. Research the best shows by reading industry magazines and visiting online forums where people in your sector are talking.

Trade show tactics

Before the event

- Negotiate a good deal – if you're prepared to wait it out, the best deals on stands can be had days before the event is starting. The closer the date, the better the price you'll negotiate as the sales team hurry to get a full house.

- Tell people you're going – circulate news that you'll be at the event through online networks (giving your location or stand number) and issue a press release if you're doing something newsworthy at the event, maybe launching a new product, having a guest appearance, running a competition, etc.

At the event

- Be clear on the offer – determine what you are selling at the show and let this be consistent across show materials; from pop-up stands to flyers. Be creative with the stand to keep costs low. Pop-up banners can be bought for £45 each from companies like Demonprint (**www.demonprint.co.uk**). Consider offering a supply of mouth-watering refreshments and branded accessories like pens, bags and t-shirts which can be ordered from companies like Vistaprint (**www.vistaprint.co.uk**) or Instantprint (**www.instantprint.co.uk**).

- Collect data – find ways to collect attendees' names and details. Offer a prize in exchange for business cards or take details in exchange for a follow-up information pack or offer. Some events also offer the facility to scan the details from the delegates' badges (for a fee).

- Take friends/family – invite a supportive team. If you're busy talking to a potential customer, you'll want others on the stand who can be doing the same. If there's time, get to know the exhibitors around you.

- Be prepared – wear comfortable shoes, bring some spare clothes and pack your lunch; if you're busy there may not be time to spend buying food and drink!

After the event

- Follow-up – within a couple of days of returning from the show, contact the people who expressed interest so that interest can be turned into sales.

- Plan ahead – if the show delivered a good return, contact the organisers and ask to be considered for a speaking slot or higher profile at the next event, and confirm your willingness to be a case study testimonial story in any post-show promotion.

Become an expert

If you have a special knowledge or experience, set yourself up as an expert in your field and the media will come knocking on your door. Here are eight ways in which you can promote your expertise.

1. Publish a book

Become a published author on your special topic. Utilise the book as a business development tool, taking copies to events, and offering free and downloadable versions to potential customers. Being an author lends you credibility and gives customers information and insight. Get in touch with publishers and agents via *The Writer's & Artist's Yearbook*, or self-publish:

- Blurb | **www.blurb.com**

- Lulu | **www.lulu.com**

- Ubyu | **www.ubyubooks.com**

Christopher Hughes has become an expert, entrepreneur and author through his football training business.

CASE STUDY

Name: **Christopher Hughes** | Business: **Little Legends**

Christopher worked in children's football training from the age of 16 but struggled to make a living from it, working several jobs on the side to make ends meet. After realising the only coaching franchises available to buy into were far too expensive, he decided to make the leap and start his own business.

At the age of just 21, Christopher used a £5k Start Up Loan to launch Little Legends, a pre-school football play programme for children under four that incorporates learning with football training. He now runs the classes in nurseries, pre-schools and weekend clubs, basing the lessons around innovative real-life situations, such as filling up £20 of petrol by kicking the ball 20 times. Little Legends has now expanded to 30 nurseries and employs 8 weekend coaches, and Christopher is launching a book with a training programme for older children, as well as setting up football charities in deprived areas he works in.

2. Present yourself

Put yourself forward to speak at events (consider asking for a fee and/or costs to be covered) or suggest being a satellite speaker, where you are beamed in via video link-up, so saving the effort and expense of travel. Invite customers and prospects and make the presentation openly available via SlideShare or Prezi.

- SlideShare | **www.slideshare.net**
- Prezi | **www.prezi.com**

3. Host a webinar

Share your expertise or demonstrate a process by hosting a webinar or visual presentation where a live audience can see you and interact. Achieve this via platforms such as GoToMeeting, GoToWebinar and WebEx, and remember to host it at a time that suits your target audience.

- GoToMeeting | **www.gotomeeting.com**

- GoToWebinar | **www.gotomeeting.com/webinar**
- WebEx | **www.webex.co.uk**

4. Produce a film

Maybe the word 'film' is a little ambitious but why not create your own video content and have a sponsored series of guides (or other content) that can be uploaded to video sharing sites such as YouTube, Vimeo and eHow?

- YouTube | **www.youtube.com**
- Vimeo | **www.vimeo.com**
- eHow | **www.ehow.co.uk**

5. Broadcast a podcast

For customers who like to listen to what you have to say at a time that suits them, upload a podcast with top tips, interviews and your thoughts of the day. Make it available on your site, iTunes and Podcast Alley to be sure of a wide audience.

- Submit a podcast to the iTunes store | **www.apple.com/itunes/podcasts**
- Podcast Alley | **www.podcastalley.com**

6. Deliver training

Whether your skill is in embroidering handmade shoes or developing stylish websites, your knowledge could be shared with others. Rather than seeing this as surrendering intelligence to potential competitors, offer instruction you're comfortable with that will create fans and followers who will learn from you, buy from you and, critically, encourage others to do the same. Check out platforms GoToTraining, WebEx and Blackboard, encourage contacts to sign up and then after the demonstration you have a chance to follow up with a group of new contacts.

- GoToTraining | **www.gotomeeting.com/fec/training/online_training**

- WebEx WebTraining | **www.webex.co.uk**
- Blackboard | **www.blackboard.com**

7. Develop an app

Take your content and make an iPhone app. Turn to browser-based platforms such as AppMmakr; "AppMakr can be used by anyone with existing content and fans or customers to reach; bloggers/writers, business owners, website owners... ".

You can either set a list price to make sales via the App Store or make it available free of charge.

- AppMakr | **www.appmakr.com**

8. Form groups

Encourage others to discuss, debate and contribute to your content by forming groups utilising social media platforms such as Facebook, LinkedIn and Ning. Bonding interested people to each other will bond them ever closer to you, the content creator and group host.

- Facebook | **www.facebook.com**
- LinkedIn | **www.linkedin.com**
- Ning | **www.ning.com**

> **BE EVERYWHERE:** *Keep in touch with existing customers via a newsletter and reach out to the new by making regular appearances at events, on other people's websites and blogs, in newspapers and magazines, and on radio and TV. Write to the magazines and radio stations that ask people to send in their story. It's a free way to get coverage. The more you're covered, the more you'll be invited to speak and comment, and before you know it, you'll be everywhere!*

Price point

These options will raise your profile but you can also generate revenue from them. Your options are:

- make your content and knowledge available at no charge to customers, to build your reputation as the go-to person and place for a particular product or service

- charge for access/downloads/viewing and turn your micropublishing activity into a revenue stream in its own right.

This is something you can assess over time. Start with a mix of charged-for and free content, ensure you're providing good value and incentives for your community to remain interested and engaged, and the options to introduce charged-for content will increase.

Embrace social media

Thanks to social media, there have never been so many tools to promote our businesses free of charge. According to research company Nielsen, the world now spends over 110 billion minutes on social networks and blogs per month. That's 22% of all time online, or one in every four and a half minutes. Embrace this and your business will become known. Here are the key tools to use and, crucially, how best to use them.

Facebook

Facebook has over 1 billion users worldwide, so if you need to be where your customers are, there's a good chance some of them will be there!

You can list on Facebook for free and/or advertise on the site and select target audience based on location, sex, age and interests. As an advertiser, you control how much you want to spend and set a daily budget. The minimum budget is US $1.00 (63p) a day. After designing your ad(s), decide for how long you want the campaign to run and whether you want to be charged for the number of clicks you receive (CPC – charge per click) or the number of times your ad is displayed. Visit **www.facebook.com**, create an account, invite friends and contacts to join your group and get promoting.

- **Cost**: free (ads are charged-for)

Twitter

Visit **www.twitter.com**, create an account, follow friends and contacts (and their followers) and get tweeting.

- **Cost**: free

How to be a success on Twitter

Twitter expert Mark Shaw (**@markshaw**) shares his four top tips that will have you tweeting like a pro:

1. "Be committed. Add a good photo, perhaps a bespoke background, your URL and an interesting bio. Try and differentiate yourself and make sure the bio contains keywords so that others can find you.

2. Be consistent. Show up each day and tweet, even if time is short. It's more important to do a small amount each day than lots one day and then nothing for a week or so.

3. Be interesting. Try and tweet three types of messages: social chit-chat; the sharing of resources, links, tools, info, ideas and opinions; and tweets that answer questions which demonstrate your knowledge. Aim for a good balance.

4. Be interested. Engage with others by answering questions and joining in. Find conversations to enter into via **search.twitter.com** and retweet (RT) other people's messages if they are of interest to you and your followers. It's not about selling things but it is all about building your brand and credibility."

Instagram

Join **www.instagram.com** and promote yourself visually by uploading photos of you and your products or service, and maybe even a few shots of happy customers. The site also carries video clips so you can show:

- events you host, speak at, or attend

- products you make (the finished product) as well as images of the production process

- happy customers wearing/using/enjoying your products and services

- your workspace

- your family (if you – and they – feel comfortable showing your personal side).

You can also easily pull the photos into your blog and social media pages.

- **Cost**: free (option to upgrade to a pro account which is a paid-for package)

LinkedIn

Referring to itself as "the world's largest professional network", LinkedIn has over 100 million members in 200-plus countries. Visit **www.linkedin.com**, create an account and start connecting with contacts and finding new ones. Form LinkedIn groups around your specialist subject.

- **Cost**: free (option to upgrade to a business account, which is a paid-for package)

YouTube

YouTube is the world's most popular online video community, with 24 hours of video uploaded every minute. Start your own business channel for free, and upload videos profiling you and your work.

Create an account (**www.youtube.com/create_account**), start a channel (advice via YouTube video!), and start broadcasting to the world. You can give each of your videos a name and assign keywords to it to help with searching, plus you can have a short description of your company on your profile page. Again, these clips are very easy to add to your website, and they help keep the content fresh and interesting.

- **Cost**: free

Pinterest

Pinterest is a virtual pinboard that lets users organise and share the beautiful things they find on the web. Big brands and small businesses have taken to Pinterest to pin pictures of their products to virtual 'pinboards'. More powerfully, customers are pinning their favourite products – and doing some of the marketing work for them!

- **Cost**: free

TOTAL BUDGET REQUIRED FOR ONLINE PROMOTION: £0

CASE STUDY

Name: **Zara Khalique** | Business: **Keep It Bright**

Zara Khalique launched a clothing company from her council house bedroom. Her clothes have gone on to be worn by stars like Ariana Grande, Miley Cyrus and Miranda Kerr.

Zara started making clothes as a hobby when she was 13-years-old and the business idea came from her own personal development.

"As a lot of teenagers do, I struggled to deal with things. I met a friend online who was a bit of a positive mentor. That helped me realise that the way you think changes everything and that saved my life. I want other people to come to that realisation.

I wanted to put positive thinking and clothing together. That's when I started my brand. It was more of a mission. I go out and put positive messages everywhere. It grew from there through word of mouth. Back then it wasn't a cool thing among young people. The negative stuff was glamorised."

When she started, Zara had no support or funding. She was making T-shirts, hoodies and other items from whatever she could scrape together.

"I was literally making things in my bedroom. I'd sell one thing to a friend and then buy more stuff. It all relied on word-of-mouth marketing, I didn't do any paid marketing until last year. The messages resonate with people, so they tell each other."

Khalique has 69,000 followers on her Keep It Bright Instagram account. She models a lot of the product photos herself and her social media accounts are full of positive advice.

"Ariana Grande and Miley Cyrus wear my stuff consistently. They just followed me on Instagram. A friend was followed by them for her art and they sent her one of my books. It's word of mouth. The only time I've given stuff to people in person is Ed Sheeran. I gave him some T-shirts in 2012.

They can get anything they want in the world and they chose to wear my stuff, which is mad. They're real people and the messages resonate. Miley and Ariana have gone through so much s**t. They are just 20-year-olds too."

Keep It Bright has remained a founder-owned business with no staff, in spite of expanding into kids clothing, homewear, and books.

"I'm literally a person doing a thing and it keeps getting bigger. I just want to reach a lot of people. I want to grow organically. People have told me to do different things with marketing. Fair enough you can get bigger quicker but I want to see how far I can go just by myself."

The consistency of the brand and the message behind it have powered the business forward. Zara said people starting new businesses need to have self belief.

"Self belief is so important. I don't mean in a delusional way. I've followed my heart. I've gone with trusting my gut. Practice makes perfect, you can teach yourself anything these days. We're so fortunate to be able to Google anything and get an answer.

From sewing to your accounts, there are so many amazing tools. Make the most of that! There's nothing to hold you back nowadays. The limitations are in your mind."

Zara's now 28 years old. Keep It Bright has received international international press attention, won a string of awards and exported around the world.

Measure the results

Time to measure what's working and what's not. Measure media and press mentions through signing up to Google Alerts – and you'll be pleased to know there's a whole host of tools that are free to use and will show real-time results for what's working on your site.

Google Analytics offers intelligence on your website traffic and marketing effectiveness: **www.google.com/analytics**

There are other analytics options:

- Alexa – web traffic metrics, site demographics and top URL listings: **www.alexa.com**

- Clicky – monitors and analyses your site traffic in real time: **www.getclicky.com**

- Opentracker – gather and analyse web stats and monitor online visitors: **www.opentracker.net**

- StatCounter – an invisible web tracker and hit counter that offers data in real time: **www.statcounter.com**

Hopefully what you will see is an upward curve of visitors and time spent on the site.

If you're selling anything, then hopefully this means more sales. If your site is the business, this means you're in a strong position to attract advertisers and begin doing affiliate deals.

> **MONKEYING AROUND:** *Run a poll with, for example, Wufoo (***www.wufoo.com***) or Survey Monkey (***www.surveymonkey.com***). Both are free to use, then publish the results via a press release and online. The media loves good polls!*

Look out, in particular, for the sources of your traffic (which are your highest referring sites) and your most popular pages. You can see days where your site receives spikes in visitor levels (and track this back to marketing) and measure if visitors are spending longer periods on the site and which times are popular, e.g. weekends, evenings, lunchtimes, etc.

PART III. Grow

With marketing and sales underway, you are
getting known and making money. Now it's
time to grow your profits by outsourcing,
keeping the business in balance, staying
on top of cash flow and getting some good
support.

13. Attract Customers Back

You are making sales via your site and developing a strong community of fans and followers. Give visitors and customers a reason to return with content that is regularly updated.

If you have a blog, try to post regularly, and if you're selling, keep the product range updated. Give your site some TLC each day, as fresh content will attract visitors who want to see what's new and will also appeal to the trawling web spiders who determine search engine results.

User-generated content

Encourage your site visitors to get to know each other through a forum or comment boxes. Before you know it, a sense of community will develop and visitors will log on each day to find out who's saying what and what's happening with whom.

Exclusive offers

Extend offers to your existing customers, readers or members that will tempt them back. This offer could be conditional on customers referring a friend: that way your customer returns to the site with others in tow. Add to this with a badge of honour; design an icon that visitors can display on their own site to show their affiliation with you. It was a 'Made in Britain' badge that led to increased sales for Brian Watt and his hot chocolate business.

Guest appearances

Invite special guests to appear on your site via guest blog posts, hosting a webchat or a featured interview.

Keep in touch

Communicate all these good and sticky things to your users through a regular e-newsletter powered by sites such as MailChimp (**www.mailchimp.com**), Constant Contact (**www.constantcontact.com**) or AWeber Communications (**www.aweber. com**).

Email marketing: keep it clean, keep it simple, keep it relevant

Email marketing works best when it is targeted. This means keeping your lists clean and organising them according to previous customer contact. A well-segmented list means you can send more frequent campaigns, ensuring a steady flow of business, without worrying about clogging up inboxes. Keep your email designs clean and simple – making it easier for your customer to make informed buying decisions in a snap.

CASE STUDY

Name: **Brian Watt** | Business: **Sloane's Hot Chocolate**

Brian Watt's bright idea was to create a high-end hot chocolate recipe. The mould-breaking pearls challenged the sugary, powdered brands that dominated the market.

> "We looked at the products we had here and saw an opportunity in hot chocolate. Coffee and tea had exploded but chocolate was going backwards. The problem was there was no innovation and excitement to the category.
>
> We produce a completely different product because we make it. It's not sugary powder it's chocolate pearls that we do by hand with machines. We put more coco in the products – up to 77%."

Hot chocolate was a small part of the business when they had the idea. The team needed to create a new brand that could champion the product.

> "When you're doing branding it helps to have some kind of anchor. What we had was Sir Hans Sloane. He created the product around 1690 and was the first to bring coca plants back to Europe.
>
> We used that to develop our brand proposition. It was a journey to find the elements that resonate with consumers. We've gone through a couple of brand designs. Our mission is to make hot chocolate lovers happy. That's why the logo has a heart. People like that story. They like the history, that backs up the whole premium proposition."

The company was making small amounts, but the level of demand quickly became unsustainable. *The Times* wrote about the business, causing retailers to get in touch.

> "When the breakthrough came – Tesco and Morrisons loved the product – we had to buy new equipment. Knowing whether to outsource manufacturing or spend the money was a tough call.
>
> I'm not saying making it yourself is easy. A couple of suppliers let me down in the last few weeks and we've been working weekends and into the night to get orders out. But doing our own manufacturing has helped us take advantage of opportunities like developing new packs for an American buyer."

Manufacturing in the UK has become a big part of their brand and helped the business expand overseas.

> "A couple of international contacts said: 'why don't you put a Union Jack on the pack?'. I thought it was a bit naff at the start but it worked really well. We started with the one we do abroad and now we do all of them. Harrods said it made such a difference."

Sloane's now distributes in the USA, Canada, Australia, Dubai, Singapore and Ireland, and 40% of sales are exports. They're on track to reach £1m turnover for the first time this year.

14. Focus On What You Do Best and Outsource the Rest

The business is growing, time is your most precious resource and you are in need of help. The quickest and most affordable place to get it is from other companies with whom you can partner to get projects done, as well as from expert advisers and mentors who will offer advice on how the business can continue to grow.

With outsourcing you can free yourself up to dedicate your attention to sales, strategy or whatever the business activity is that you do best. My advice to all businesses is always: *focus on what you do best and outsource the rest.*

What can be outsourced and to whom?

Admin

Hire a VA (virtual assistant) to do the admin tasks you don't want or don't have the time to do. Find skilled VAs via sites such as:

- Worldwide101 | **worldwide101.com**

and

- Time Etc | **www.timeetc.com**

Accounts

Unless you are in the accountancy business, this is almost a must to be outsourced. Monthly payroll, accounts, VAT returns and corporate tax returns all take time and it's time you can't afford or simply don't have. A cost/benefit analysis is likely to show that it's cheaper to outsource to a qualified accountant. Ask around for recommendations of accountants in your area who deliver a quality service at a competitive cost and are registered with the Institute of Chartered Accountants for England and Wales (ICAEW). As mentioned earlier, you can connect with and benefit from free consultations with ICAEW accountants via Enterprise Nation (**www.enterprisenation.com**).

PR, marketing and design

Outsource your PR to a specialist who can be pitching and promoting the business whilst you're at work. Find skilled professionals on directory sites such as Enterprise Nation (**www.enterprisenation.com**) and PeoplePerHour (**www.peopleperhour.com**).

Sales

Hire a sales expert to make calls, set up appointments and attend trade shows. Find these professionals online, contact telemarketing companies that offer outbound sales calls as a service, or look at sales specialists such as Winning Sales (**www.winningsales.co.uk**).

Customer service

Looking after customers is vital, but even that can be outsourced. Get Satisfaction's tagline is "people-powered customer service" – it provides a web-hosted platform, much like a forum, where customers can ask questions, suggest improvements, report a problem or give praise. This and other online customer satisfaction tools can save you time and money by having the power of the crowd take care of customer questions!

- Get Satisfaction | **www.getsatisfaction.com**
- Zen Desk | **www.zendesk.com**

IT

Spending too many hours trying to fix a single IT problem? Outsource the hassle and save your time, money and blood pressure. Find IT professionals online via Enterprise Nation. **www.enterprisenation.com**

Steps to successful outsourcing

Do the groundwork

Spend some time working on the task yourself so you've built foundations before handing it over to someone else. For example, if you outsource sales then have a ready-made contacts list and some open doors that the specialist can build on, rather than starting from scratch. This will make it more cost-effective for you and means that they hit the ground running.

Be clear on the brief

Having spent some time doing the task yourself, you will have a clear idea of the brief. Back to the example of outsourcing sales, if you've spent 6–12 months sourcing leads and making contacts, you'll have a much clearer idea of the type of work the specialist should do.

The clearer the brief, the better the results.

Take your time

And take references. Spend time evaluating the specialists in the market and, if you can, talk to their existing clients. Do they have the industry experience you're after? Will they represent your brand in a professional manner? Have they delivered a good job for other clients? When an outsourced arrangement works well, the partner becomes part of your team – so choose them as carefully as you would choose an employee.

Let go!

Outsourcing means having to let go a little. Someone else becomes accountable for these results. Embrace this rather than resist it. As the business owner you remain in ultimate control but the expert will need their own space in which to flourish. Outsourcing can save you time and help make you money. Finding the right partner, on the right terms, will make you feel like a new and liberated person.

Form teams

Once you've chosen your outsourced partner(s), it's important to keep in regular contact and work together as a team. There are a number of online project management and collaboration tools to help you stay on top of projects and in control of the company.

- Basecamp | **www.basecamp.com** is the project management tool we rely on at Enterprise Nation. This is a top-class product that allows you to create projects, invite people to view them, upload files and make comments. It's effective online project management that can be accessed from anywhere.

- Share documents via Google Docs | **docs.google.com**. You can edit on the move, choose who accesses documents and share changes in real time.

- Huddle | **www.huddle.com** offers simple and secure online workspaces. Huddle is hosted, so there's no software to download and it's free to get started.

Solutions to enable group-talk

- GoToMeeting | **www.gotomeeting.com**

Work with anyone, anywhere with this easy to use online meeting tool.

- Trello | **www.trello.com**

Share and record action lists.

- Powwownow | **www.powwownow.co.uk**

Free conference calling at 'open access' level. Priced packages available.

Form partnerships

If relationships develop, you may decide to form a partnership. Consider writing a partnership agreement as your pre-nup in business. At the outset of a relationship, all is good and you're excited about the potential, but it's best to be safe; have the terms written and agreed so that all parties are clear on expectations.

The following should not be taken as concrete legal advice, more of a guideline on how to draw up an agreement.

Scope of agreement

What is your partnership working to achieve? For example, "This agreement is made between Company A and Company B. The agreement is related to the generation of online advertising revenues/hosting of an event/development of a new product."

Respective responsibilities

Set out the expectations on who does what. For example, Company A will be responsible for promotion and business development and Company B will take on technical development and client care. Also include a note of how you'll keep each other briefed, maybe through the use of an online project management tool.

Finances

What will be the split in revenue, and is this before or after costs? And who owns the intellectual property of the product/service/activity? Consider including a clause that states the agreement will be reviewed in six months so that both parties can check on progress and have the right to cease the agreement if it hasn't gone as planned.

Be fair

Agreements where both parties feel that they're receiving their fair share are likely to be longer-lasting than those when one party feels embittered. Talk about this before writing and concluding the agreement. Make sure there's no resentment or sense of being exploited on either side.

Sign it!

After making the effort to produce an agreement, be sure to sign it! And then store it so that you can access it easily if the need arises.

When writing the clauses in your agreement, think about all the things that could go wrong and safeguard against them. It's a practical exercise and won't harm your newly formed business relationship but will get it off on a firm footing.

BUSINESS OWNER PLUS ONE: *When the business is at a stage to take on its first new employee, visit the 'Growing your business' section of the GOV.UK site (**www.gov.uk/growing-your-business/hire-and-train-staff**), which offers details on how to employ and your obligations as an employer over time.*

15. Keep the Business in Balance

As the business continues to grow, you will want to maintain momentum and grow at a comfortable pace. Achieve this by following what I call 'the golden triangle', which will keep you and the business in balance. This requires spending roughly a third of your time on three key things:

1. Customer care

Look after your customers by delivering a quality product or service, on time and within budget. And remember... the customer is always right!

I ask clients for feedback so that I can keep a check on what they're thinking and changes they'd like to see. It's good to know some personal details about your customers, too. (Maybe their birthday, their favourite hobby.) As you gather these details, make a quick note so you can send a birthday card on the right date, etc. Don't go overboard, but showing that you care certainly won't harm your relationship.

Offer customers good service, regular communication and an innovative line of products and services. It will stand you in good stead.

2. New business

Taking care of customers means taking care of sales. Why? Because it costs less to win business from existing customers than it does to find new ones. If customers are happy, they'll say good things about you to new and potential customers. This is called word-of-mouth marketing and achieving it is every business owner's dream!

Secure new clients through marketing, encouraging recommendations, and direct-sales calls and pitches.

3. Admin

Not as enjoyable as the first two, but it still has to be done. Keep the books in order by raising invoices in good time, being on top of cash flow, and filing tax returns and company documents on time and in order. In short, keep the finances in check and the books up-to-date.

Cash is king

In *9. Starting on a Budget and Straightforward Finance* we looked at the topic of straightforward finance and how to plan income and outgoings.

Keep an eye on the accounts so you can see how much money is in the bank, how much is owed and whether this covers your outgoings.

This is a vital part of running your business and something you will need to keep close tabs on especially at the start. Monitor this using your accounting software and online banking. It's a very well-worn phrase in business, but cash is most definitely king.

Getting paid and paying others

A key part in managing your cash flow is making sure you get paid and get paid promptly. How you get paid will depend quite a lot on the type of business you have and whether you are selling direct to customers or to other businesses. If selling directly, you will mostly be paid immediately. If you are dealing with other businesses, the chances are most will expect to pay on invoice (more on this below) and will expect a credit period in which to pay. Be prepared to offer credit terms, but be careful about how long you give, how much credit you'll allow and who you offer this to.

If you need to buy in products or services from others as part of your business, it's always worth seeing if you too can arrange credit terms with suppliers. This should help you balance payments in and out. This isn't always easy at the start and you may have to pay upfront to begin with, but it is something to ask for. Having built up a good relationship with your supplier it should be a natural next step.

Invoices

Be on time with invoicing and keep a record of amounts outstanding. Start with a simple spreadsheet with five columns labelled 'client', 'invoice amount', 'invoice number', 'date submitted' and 'date paid'.

- Your invoices should be a simple document with basic details. The less cause for question on the invoice, the faster it will be paid.

- Always find out in advance who should be named on the invoice, where it should be sent and whether you need to include any sort of order reference number. When dealing with large companies in particular, this sort of thing can make a big difference to how quickly you get paid.

- Settle invoices as promptly as you can. Your suppliers should be grateful and repay you with good service.

See the next page for an example invoice.

Hopefully your clients and customers will always pay promptly, but occasionally you might need to remind them. Do this politely and clearly. It's often sensible to send a monthly statement to a client detailing any outstanding invoices, and usually that's enough to spur them into action.

You can balance the budget with a piece of accounting software such as Xero (**www.xero.com/uk**).

Receipts

Keep business-related receipts in a place where they're easy to find. It's helpful that they're all in one place when it's time to do the VAT return. Or record as you go along with tools like Receipt Bank (**www.receipt-bank.com/uk/**).

Track your time with time-tracking software

- Cashboard | **www.getcashboard.com**

- Four Four Time | **www.fourfourtime.co.uk**

- TraxTime | **www.spudcity.com/traxtime**

Sample invoice

1. Name and address of your contact

2. The date

3. Your company address

4. Company registration and VAT number (if applicable)

5. Invoice number and client's purchase order (PO) number

6. Payment terms (e.g. payable within 30 days of receipt), and by cheque, transfer, etc.

7. A brief product description or summary of services

8. Amount owing (inclusive or exclusive of VAT, depending on whether you're registered) plus your bank payment details to allow your contact to pay by bank transfer.

9. I think it's good practice to include a cover note, too, that confirms what's being invoiced and thanks the client for their custom.

YOUR SMALL BUSINESS

Invoice

1. Attention: Joe Smith
Managing Director
A. N. Other Small Business
321 First Street
Anytown, County AB1 2CD
Date 01/12/19 **2.**

3. Your small business address
123 Second Street
Anothertown, County AB2 3CD
T 01234 567 8910
F 01234 567 8911
you@youremailaddress.com
http://www.yourwebsite.com/

4. Your company registration
VAT no. 12345678910

PROJECT TITLE: A. N. Other Small Business website
PROJECT DESCRIPTION: Redesign of business website **5.**
INVOICE NUMBER: 01
TERMS: 30 days **6.** **8.**

Description	Amount owed
Graphic design	£1,500.00
Programming	£2,000.00
Hosting	£500.00
Total	**£4,000.00**

7.

PLEASE MAKE PAYMENT BY BANK TRANSFER TO:

Bank: Your Bank, 1 High Street, Town, AB2 3CD
Account name: Your Small Business
Sort code: 01 02 03
Account: 12345678

Sincerely yours,

Your Name

16. Support

All of the success stories in this kit have spoken of the valuable support received from friends, family, advisers and experienced entrepreneurs.

Ask questions at every opportunity and build a support network. Here's where to look for people who are happy to help.

Peers

Who better to turn to than those going through the same experience as you? Visit Enterprise Nation to join the UK's most active small business community.

Mentors

Find a mentor through making a direct approach to experts, professionals and business owners you admire and respect. Or source one via accessing a loan with Start Up Loans or head out to events to find them in person.

And don't restrict yourself to one mentor! I have learnt from many people as my businesses have passed through different stages of development. My approach was to get in touch with the person I felt best placed to have the answer, take on board their views, consider my options, and then act.

In my view, the ideal mentor is someone who possesses four things:

1. experience of your industry/sector

2. the ability to listen

3. the technical skills to advise

4. a willingness to make introductions to useful contacts.

If you can find these in one person, you are very fortunate indeed.

One of the finest things a mentor can do is allow you to talk. By doing so, you often work out the answer. Sometimes you just need an experienced sounding board.

Accelerate!

And finally... if you want to give your business an extra injection and growth spurt, check out some of the 'Accelerators' launched by companies to give you space, funding and access to mentors, technology and customers.

- Wayra | **wayra.org/en**
- Accelerator Academy | **www.acceleratoracademy.com**
- The Bakery | **www.thebakerylondon.com**
- Collider 13 | **collider13.com/about**
- New Entrepreneurs Foundation | **www.newentrepreneursfoundation.co.uk**
- Entrepreneur First | **www.entrepreneurfirst.org.uk**
- TechStars | **www.techstars.com/program/locations/london**
- Microsoft BizSpark | **www.microsoft.com/BizSpark**
- GrowthAccelerator | **www.growthaccelerator.com**
- Level 39 | **www.level39.co**
- The Grocery Accelerator | **groceryaccelerator.co.uk**

The Best of Luck

You've read the stories, devoured the tips and completed the templates. It's time to take your own idea, passion, hobby or skill, and turn it into a business.

I hope what you've picked up from this kit is that regardless of your age, background or sector, if you're starting out as your own boss there's support all around. In whichever direction you turn, you'll find people to cheer you along and answer your questions; you'll find loans on offer and resources on tap.

Make the most of this support and never be afraid to seek help or approach mentors. With guidance from those who've trodden the entrepreneurial path, you will find your own way and build a future that offers financial reward and freedom in your working life.

Start-ups are most definitely the new rock stars and I see no sign of this wearing out any time soon. Big companies want to be seen alongside you and customers want to buy from you. These are good conditions in which to start a new venture.

So, now it's over to you. And even though this farewell is entitled 'Best of Luck', one of my favourite quotes is one that's well known and came from golf pro Gary Player, who said: "The harder I practise, the luckier I get."

My advice to you: go practise and get lucky!

Emma Jones | @emmaljones

How Enterprise Nation Can Help

Enterprise Nation helps thousands of people in the UK turn their good ideas into great businesses.

There's lots of free advice on our website and events, where you can get together with other start-ups and would-be entrepreneurs to learn from experience and from experts.

Find out more at **www.enterprisenation.com**.

With Thanks

To the following people who have contributed their expertise, story or tip in the compilation of this kit:

The start-ups

Emma Cranstoun | **Scrubbington's**

PJ Farr | **UK Connect**

Meenesh Mistry | **Wholey Moly**

Nisha Katona MBE | **Mowgli Street Foods**

Rebecca Linnell | **Country Dog Hotel**

Mechelle Clark | **Melt Aberdeen**

Razan Al-Sous | **Dama Cheese**

Victoria Bustard | **Plant & Play Wildlife Centre**

Christopher Hughes | **Little Legends**

Zara Khalique | **Keep It Bright**

Brian Watt | **Sloane's Hot Chocolate**